new shoes
contemporary footwear design

Sue Huey and Rebecca Proctor

new shoes
contemporary footwear design

Laurence King Publishing

Published in 2007 by Laurence King Publishing Ltd
361–373 City Road
London EC1V 1LR
United Kingdom
e-mail: enquiries@laurenceking.co.uk
www.laurenceking.co.uk

Copyright © text 2007 Sue Huey and Rebecca Proctor

A catalogue record for this book is available from the British Library.

ISBN 10: 1 85669 507 7
ISBN 13: 978 185669 507 7

Printed in China

Design Charlie Hanson
Commissioning editor Helen Evans
Project editor Catherine Hooper
Production Felicity Awdry
Copy editor Carol Franklin
Photography Esther Teichmann
Digital retoucher Matt Doyle
Stylist Lara Ferros
Set design Anna Burns
Hair and make-up Maarit Niemelson
Models Jess Craven, Camilla Thomsen, Georgina Thoms @ ICM Models;
Elcee Orlova, Phoebe Watson, Emma Jade @ IMG Models

Cover Thanks to Habitat for the bedspread (www.habitat.net), and to
Jenne O for the 'Dita V' ankle boots, see p. 74 for details.
Pages 2–3 Nicholas Kirkwood's 'Revealer' court shoe. See p. 87 for details.

contents

introduction

And as I cobble with needle and thread,
I judge the world by the way they tread
Heels worn thick and soles worn thin
Toes turned out and toes turned in,

There's food for thought in a sandal string
For prince and commoner, poor and rich,
Stand in need of the cobbler's stitch.

(*The Cobbler's Song*, chu chin chow, 1934)

From the smooth lines of the unopened box to the soft rustling of tissue paper, there are few things in life that excite women (and often men) as much as a new pair of shoes. Why do these objects hold such fascination for us? And what are the components that go to make up the perfect shoe?

In this book we present twenty-five contemporary footwear designers, who work at the forefront of the footwear industry. Each has been chosen for their innovative attitude to design and, most importantly, for their passion. It is clear that each designer approaches his or her work in a very different way, but the one factor that unites them all is their unswerving devotion to their craft and its rich heritage. This dedication equips all twenty-five designers with the knowledge and ability to drive footwear design into the future.

Primarily worn to protect our feet, the shoe will always be an intrinsically practical and necessary item of clothing. However, due to our increasing detachment from nature and ever more radical examples of footwear design (some of which are featured in this book), it is easy to forget the shoe's profound significance. Nonetheless, footwear is still chosen according to our environment, and we would no more wear wellingtons in the sunshine than sandals in the snow. In this way, shoes will always betray important clues about our habitat and our way of life.

More recently, the shoe has become an object of beauty and desire, a testament to the vision of these skilled and pioneering designers. The variety of footwear styles available today allows us all to express fully our individual tastes, and the messages communicated by our choice of shoe have surely never been greater. For example, stilettos are renowned for being both sexy and restrictive – they lengthen the leg, raise the buttocks and encourage women to walk slowly while wiggling their hips; these heels also make that familiar 'click, click' noise, which can be instantly recognized from ten paces away. Wedges bring to mind nostalgic fashions; while ballerina flats will always be considered effortlessly chic.

Making shoes or cobbling was once considered to be a lowly trade, ranking alongside the carpenter, the blacksmith and the seamstress. Today, however, the inevitable march of mass production through the footwear industry has forced us to sit up and realize (perhaps a little too late) that every hand-sewn shoe is in fact a precious object created by highly skilled and trained craftspeople.

It is not known exactly when shoemaking developed as a craft, although evidence suggests that it existed as a trade in Egypt as far back as 2000 BC. The skills, tricks and wiles of the trade have doubtless been altered and refined over the centuries, yet today's process of constructing footwear still consists of the same essential stages as it did one or even two hundred years ago.

However, the fundamental change has been in the division of labour. Until the mid-twentieth century, the actual designing of the shoe was not considered a separate artistic pursuit, rather a part of the whole cobbling process. This is a far cry from today when celebrated designers such as Christian Louboutin, Jimmy Choo and Manolo Blahník are household names, while the craftsmen who produce the shoes in factories remain anonymous.

The most significant recent development in the footwear industry has undoubtedly been the large-scale transfer of footwear production to Vietnam, India, Indonesia, Thailand and, above all, China. Implemented entirely on economic grounds, this shift is due to manufacturers who are willing to sacrifice quality for the promise of a keen workforce who will work for a fraction of Western wages. Consequently, this has meant that many of Europe's highly skilled artisan craftsmen, unable to compete with such cheap labour, have been made redundant.

There is much talk within the shoemaking industry of these Asian countries eventually taking over the entire industry, but in Italy, traditionally the most important footwear manufacturer in Europe, shoemakers have refocused on what they do best and continue to produce shoes of particularly high quality. The Italians are relentlessly meticulous and proud of their perfection in quality and craftsmanship, making shoes that are far superior to anything created in the East. It could be argued, however, that under the right conditions, the prospect of Chinese production offers a valid alternative. Each designer featured in this book tackles the problems of production differently. As consumers, we must make informed choices, which will allow the footwear industry to flourish ethically and in the right direction.

Ultimately our choice of footwear is a personal one. Shoes have the power to seduce us, move us and empower us. They can fulfil our fantasies and help us to escape from reality. The future of shoe design lies in the hands of our contemporary designers and each shoe featured on the following pages has been chosen to inspire and intrigue you with its beauty. Although each shoe is different, the common thread that links them all is their exquisite craftsmanship. This, we believe, is the key to modern luxury.

Opposite Minna Parikka's 'Sweetheart' lace-up boot. See p. 134 for details.

nicole
brundage

Revelling in descriptions such as 'devilishly ladylike', 'sensually seductive' and 'tainted by noir allure', Nicole Brundage is not the creator of ordinary footwear. Finding creativity in various sources, such as the work of fetish artist John Willie, the pin-up girls of Robert Harrison and the roles of women in different professions, epochs and cultures, Brundage loves to play with contrasts.

'Freedom versus constraint, discretion versus overstatement, eroticism versus chastity and revelation versus concealment' are the inspiration behind her designs. 'Women in essence are always being torn between contrasts,' she says, 'and for me this tension is what makes them strong and intriguing.' As a protective layer for the foot, the shoe is undoubtedly one of the most practical items of dress, and Brundage is intrigued by the way so many women choose to defy this reality. 'Despite the flagrant impracticality of stilettos, a woman will still wear them for the sheer fun of it,' she says, 'knowing that there is something powerfully seductive about her wearing them.' This juxtaposition is at the core of Brundage's work and pushes her to create footwear that blurs the boundaries between fetishism and feminism.

Brundage's distinct style combines elements of extreme modernity with unexpected references to ancient cultures and crafts, including Greek mythology and origami. 'For toes, heels and hardware, I look to geometry and cylindrical, conical, diagonal and circular shapes,' she explains. This love of contrast is apparent not only in her inspiration, but also in her choice of materials and textures. Past collections have seen matt timbers mixed with polished Perspex, and fused satin with natural-grain leathers.

With her sense of playful theatre, it is easy to see why Brundage cites Azzedine Alaia and Vivienne Westwood as design influences. Her style also flourished while studying at the Istituto Marangoni in Milan, which she attended after working with US designer Zac Posen. It was whilst working for Posen, however, that a chance opportunity arose to design his Fall 2004 collection. 'I realized then that I enjoyed all the elements implicit in a shoe, from both a design and figurative perspective, thus discovering something of a hidden fixation.' This fascination led to a new career and the successful launch of her eponymously titled brand.

Despite being a relatively recent addition to the footwear firmament, Texan-born Brundage is already well established in her home country, as well as winning over her European counterparts. Her plans for the brand are ambitious, but she hopes to continue to push into different cultural markets, while trying to bring something new to the industry. She says, 'I think for shoes to be really special, inexplainably "wow", they must appeal to a woman's imagination, playfulness and need to feel sensual, while simultaneously addressing her sense of practicality and sophistication. Few shoes accomplish this.'

Opposite Made from olive-green patent leather, the 'Thomasina' is a modern-day Mary Jane. See p. 12 for details.

'Shoes must appeal to a woman's imagination.'

Nicole Brundage

Page 10, top left This peep-toe, two-tone Mary Jane is a fabulously feminine version of a traditional men's Oxford. The flesh-coloured nappa and black patent leather are held together with minimal stitching and the shoe has a 95mm heel. **bottom left** With its discreet 10mm forepart platform, square-cut vamp, extended strap fastening and extended heel top line, the 'Thomasina' is a modern Mary Jane. The shoe also features an almond toe shape, oversized leather-covered buckle and 95mm heel.

Page 10, right and page 11 This Victorian-inspired equestrian boot in chocolate-coloured calf has a covered 10mm forepart platform and 95mm heel. The upper features a zip-front fastening and three decorative lace-up ties. **This page** Original design sketches showing different angles of a sandal with a 100mm cylindrical heel that is part-wood, part-Perspex.

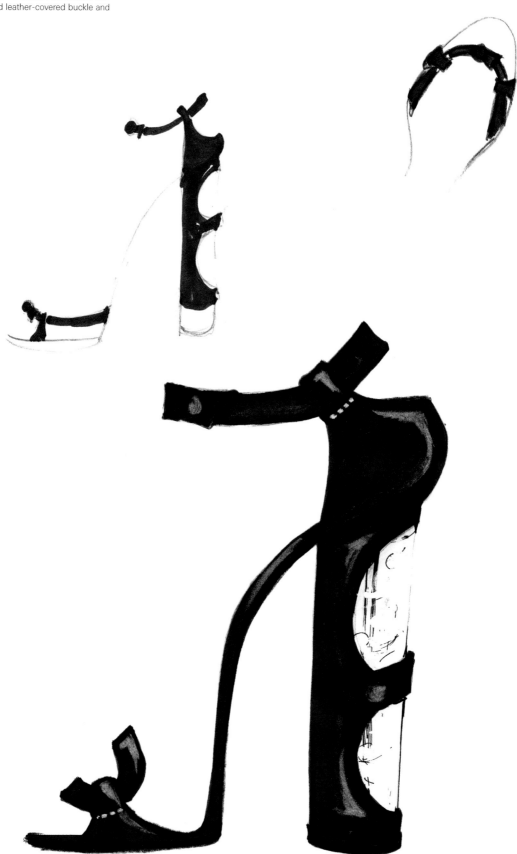

This page, top left A cross between an Oxford and a Mary Jane, this shoe sketch has a double strap, heavy contrast stitching, a covered 15mm forepart platform and a 100mm heel. **top right** Sketch for a T-strap sandal with a 95mm heel and square toe shape. The toes are revealed through a square opening on the upper.

bottom left Design sketch for a strappy sandal with gimped trim loops. **bottom right** Design for a strappy sandal with a 95mm heel, heavy contrast stitching and riveted edges.

Peep-toe patent and nappa shoe.
See p. 12 for details.

marco censi

Marco Censi describes his work as 'footwear for the modern-day dandy', a description that is particularly apt for a designer who enjoys breaking all the codes of traditional menswear and reinventing them with humour and intelligence. His witty designs are purposefully ironic, referencing traditional design details, but reworking them with a new aesthetic functionalism.

The basis of Censi's approach is derived from the traditional school of shoemaking. He favours 'a low-tech attitude with no limitations or prejudices' and chooses quality craftsmanship over machine-made convenience. The results are elaborately detailed shoes, painstakingly finished by hand, but crafted from simple materials like split leather or oil-treated canvas.

Deliberately refusing to restrict himself with materials, Censi cheerfully mixes luxury leathers with cheaper man-made materials. He confesses to having a huge admiration for furnishing fabrics and admits, 'I especially love antique-style brocades, which I use the wrong side up'. This original feature adds a warm, textural finish that complements Censi's trademark lean, tapered lines.

The defining motif in Censi's work is a delicate embroidered rose, reminiscent of the markings on an old cowboy boot or old-fashioned table linen. The flower can often be found, peeping out, tone on tone, on the upper or sole of a shoe.

As for his other influences, Censi confesses to having a penchant for people watching. 'I enjoy observing people on the street....I especially like the old Italian ladies and gentlemen who are incredibly elegant. They always dress with a very personal attitude, much more so than the younger generation who today always dress the same.'

Censi has always been surrounded by fashion. His mother was a costumier who owned a boutique on the beachfront of their small tourist town, just outside Rome. He explains that it was regularly frequented by 'glamorous ladies on holiday during the 1960s and 1970s'.

On completing a degree in jewelry design in 1983, Censi was invited by the editorial team of *Donna* magazine to attend the first Fashion and Industrial Design course at the prestigious Domus Academy in Milan. It was here that he developed his true passion for shoes.

A chance meeting in 1990 with Guillaume Hinfray (Censi's design partner for the last fifteen years, see p. 60) sealed his fate. Together the two created *Newtrends/Walking*, an innovative trend book for shoes, and spent the next decade developing their technical skills and business acumen. The pair simultaneously acted as consultants for Costume National, Sergio Rossi, Premiata and RAS, and were eventually appointed head designers for both men's and women's shoes at Bottega Veneta and Salvatore Ferragamo.

In 2001, they decided to create their own brand Ameratsau, which was followed by Guillaume Hinfray in 2004 and, finally, Marco Censi, their line specializing in men's footwear, in 2006. In the future, Censi aspires to set up a home from home: 'My secret dream is to open up my own store, an old-style, cosy, intimate place for customers, like me, who are tired of big ultra-modern concept stores.'

Opposite Slip-on loafer. See p. 18 for details.

Slip-on loafer in velvet brocade and chocolate
nappa leather with nappa tassel trim.

18

This page Dark blue Chelsea boot with circular zip fastening and elegant elongated toe made from the softest suede.
Page 20, left and page 21 Tan nubuck, lace-up Derby shoe with an elongated toe and minimal stitching. The slightly contrasting leather lace is a subtle but stylish addition.
Page 20, right Toffee-coloured slip-on leather loafer with apron construction, leather-covered chain hardware and elongated toe shape.

'My work is footwear for the modern-day dandy.'

Marco Censi

Opposite Deep mahogany Monk-style shoe with extended wrap-around strap fastening and elongated toe.
This page, right Original sketch for a wing-tip Oxford. **right middle** Design for a slip-on loafer with an oversized buckle and strap fastening. **right bottom** Sketch for a Chelsea boot with diagonal elastic inserts from the sole to the top line and an elongated toe. **below** Ankle boot in coffee leather with wrap-over lace fastening and elongated toe.

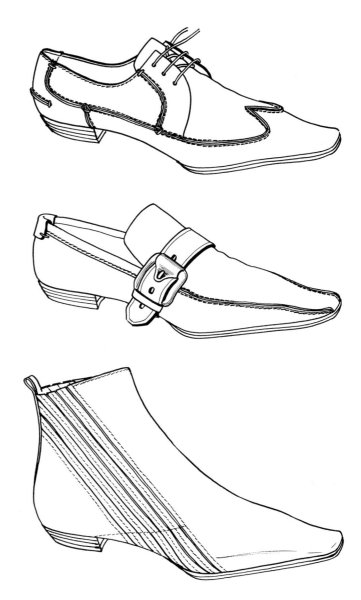

adele
clarke

'I hate the idea of being a flash in the pan,' says Adele Clarke. 'I think accessories should be things that you treasure and bring out time and time again.' Having worked in the footwear industry for over ten years, with such prestigious clients as Asprey, DKNY, Hussein Chalayan and Tanner Krolle, Clarke can rest assured that there is little chance her work will be forgotten.

Clarke's distinctive style, which marries experimental constructions with high-quality materials, is highly regarded in the industry, with fellow footwear designer Rupert Sanderson (see p. 148) describing her as 'one of the finest shoe designers in London'. The reason for Clarke's success lies in the fact that she designs footwear for strong and thoughtful women, just like herself.

'It is very important to me as a designer not to sell out,' says Clarke. 'I want to make sure that I am making the best possible product. For me, that is one that will last and one that will bring pleasure to those who wear it. You have to remember that shoes are an adjunct to everything else. You wear them, they don't wear you.' This uncompromising attitude strikes a chord with women who refuse to support the disposable nature of high-street trends, opting instead for sustainable products that will last a lifetime. Her designs, although undeniably contemporary, exude a classic grace and elegance that transcend fashion.

Clarke began her footwear career by creating shoes for fashion designer Hussein Chalayan. Having studied Fashion at Central Saint Martin's in London, she spent two seasons working with Chalayan's stylist, gradually becoming 'more and more involved with his footwear'. Her fascination for the discipline encouraged Clarke to complete the Royal College of Art's MA in Footwear, during which time she

continued working with Chalayan and eventually graduated into making and designing his entire footwear range: Adele Clarke for Hussein Chalayan.

When Chalayan's revolutionary designs required equally radical footwear, Clarke responded by producing skilful and experimental collections, which complemented his apparel perfectly. For instance, when Hussein based an entire collection on mirror images, she created pairs of shoes that were the mirror image of each other.

After leaving Chalayan, Clarke created her own line, Adele Clarke, which has a very different feel from her previous work. What remains the same, however, is the exquisite craftsmanship, considered silhouettes and use of luxury materials that have become synonymous with Clarke's name.

Although work on her own label is temporarily suspended, Clarke remains optimistic about the future and is currently concentrating on building her business 'the right way'. As part of this process she has been revisiting her previous designs. 'It's funny going through my archive,' she says, 'seeing all the pieces that I've made. They are like old friends visiting me again from the past and it's made me realize that I'll go on making shoes forever, regardless of whether someone pays me or not.'

Opposite Black, yellow, chocolate and flesh-coloured strappy sandal with an 80mm high heel and black patent mudguard, which cups the toes.

'You wear shoes, they don't wear you.'

Adele Clarke

Previous spread Adele Clarke for Hussein Chalayan sandal with a 110mm leather-covered block heel. The sandal has a classic lasted construction with soft pleated grey jersey crossing on the upper and knotting at the ankle.
Below Working sketches showing range building and development.

This page, top Luxurious gold nappa and hand-painted python court shoes with multi-peep toe, hidden mudguard and 80mm stacked-leather heels. middle Pavement grey suede and natural python court shoes with punched apron, whip stitching and 105mm covered Louis heels. bottom These technically challenging court shoes are made up of a three-dimensional patchwork of black, charcoal-grey and metallic-black nappa. The striking design also features a 105mm Louis heel and domed round toe.

29

Pull-on maroon nappa boot with mudguard detail, 50mm block heel and almond toe shape.

diego
dolcini

Diego Dolcini designs shoes that are made not only to be worn but also to be collected as items of unique beauty and pieces of sculpture. Originally a student of architecture, he was driven to create footwear after being inspired by the many similarities between the disciplines: 'Shoes are objects that take a structure,' he says. 'In their case, the structure is the human body – the most beautiful architectural work in the world!'

Employing the rigid, geometric shapes learned from architecture and product design, Dolcini flirts dangerously with fetish styling featuring high feminine heels, and more formal styles with low and medium-height heels. He also revels in the theatrical nature of footwear, as shown in his 'Millennium Kit', a product launched in Autumn/Winter 99/00 that allows the wearer to 'transform' her footwear with the aid of a luxurious set of accessories. Simple boots or sandals for day can be converted to customized boots or jewelled shoes for evening.

Born in Naples, Italy, Dolcini studied architecture at the Milan Polytechnic and Fine Arts school in Bologna. Following his degree, he was awarded a scholarship to study a Masters at the prestigious Domus Academy in Milan, where he was immediately drawn to footwear design and began an intense period of renewed study.

He has collaborated with several leading brands in the industry including Bruno Magli, Emilio Pucci and Bulgari. From 2001 to 2004, Dolcini also joined forces with Tom Ford as the creative director of men's and women's shoes at Gucci, where he was responsible for the brand's iconic bamboo-heeled court shoes.

Dolcini launched a line in his own name in 1994, during a time of intense and very rapid stylistic growth at the heart of the Italian shoe-manufacturing industry. At that time, Dolcini came face to face with all the major production problems of the factory and gained an in-depth knowledge of footwear craftsmanship. Thanks to his architecture training, Dolcini was able to reinterpret the problems in a new and original way, combining the technical innovation of production processes with the tradition of handmade work. He continues to work with the very best artisan shoe manufacturers – who are usually based in the esteemed Emilia Romagna district of his native Italy.

Due to the maverick and highly luxurious nature of his work, Dolcini has become renowned for creating top quality footwear for a very select and elite clientele. His footwear is produced in deliberately limited numbers and is frequently shown at the haute couture shows in Paris and collected by his many high-profile clients.

Opposite Gold-studded almond-toe court shoe with a 100mm stacked-leather heel.

'A shoe is an object that takes a structure.'

Diego Dolcini

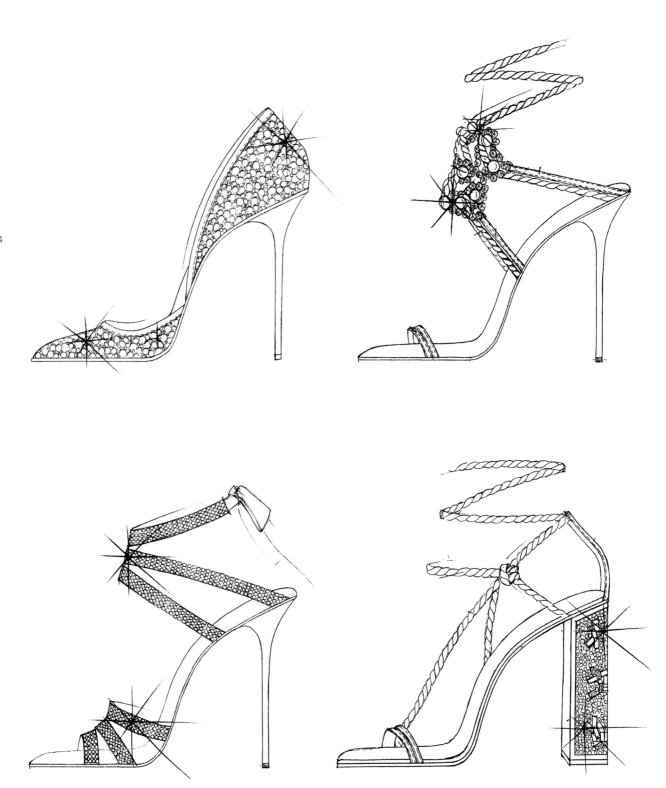

Opposite Original sketches showing a range of highly decorative evening styles.
This page, left Decadent strappy sandal with gold rope, Swarovski crystals, pearls and glass beads. The sandal has a 100mm gold stiletto heel and an almond last shape. **below** Crystal-encrusted chunky heel sandal with black satin rope straps.
Overleaf Gold python and suede court shoe with a 100mm block heel and almond toe.

finsk

'My shoes are more like design objects rather than footwear,' says Finnish designer Julia Lundsten, whose shoes meld strong architectural shapes and butter-soft leathers with striking wooden heels. All too often wooden heels are incredibly conventional, ignoring the beauty of the material itself; but Lundsten's unique style has drawn critical acclaim from all over the world and has even succeeded in captivating legendary footwear designer Manolo Blahník. 'Her work is like nothing anybody is doing at the moment…exquisite, divine and perfect,' he says. In fact, Blahník was so taken with Lundsten's architectural forms that, while she was studying for her Masters degree in Footwear at London's Royal College of Art, he presented her with the prestigious Manolo Blahník Award two years in a row.

Lundsten's interest in design was sparked at an early age when she spent her summers touring Scandinavia, visiting buildings with her architect father and interior designer mother. This experience has clearly had a lasting effect on her as she likens her shoe designs to buildings and chairs: 'a shoe is like a chair, the heel and sole being the chair legs and the upper the seat'.

She initially studied fashion design but rejected the discipline because she did not like the way that the body plays such a fundamental part in how a finished garment looks. 'The shape and look of clothing changes completely with each body and I was always intrigued by shoes as they are related to a woman and her body, but the shape is a shape in itself and it doesn't really change with different "foot shapes".' As soon as she started concentrating fully on shoes, Lundsten knew that she had finally found 'the right combination of fashion and architecture'.

In 2005, Lundsten launched her label Finsk, meaning Finnish. She is constantly testing and developing new solutions and details for her wooden heels, which are like pieces of skilfully designed furniture. She also uses exotic Brazilian hardwoods, which are coated with surface treatments and finishes drawn from her native architecture. 'I love wood as a material,' she says, 'it has so many beautiful characteristics that you can bring out.'

The techniques and finishing processes that she uses are also frequently derived from furniture design. They include an innovative wood veneer technique that allows dye to penetrate deep into the grain, so that even when the surface wears out, the colour can still be seen. Such veneers are perfect for creating high-quality surfaces, which are able to withstand wear, and ideal for shoe heels as well as the more obvious applications for flooring and furniture.

As well as working on her own line, Lundsten has taken care of New York designer Mary Ping's footwear collection since Fall/Winter 2005/2006. She also designs for the British high street, acting as a consultant for Reiss, Kurt Geiger and Top Shop, among others.

Opposite Black leather thong sandal with decorative looped thong detail and ankle-wrap fastening.

This page Original sketches showing front, side and rear views of Finsk's sculptural-style shoes.

Opposite, top Two views of a black leather peep-toe court shoe with decorative looped upper and an eye-catching set-in Brazilian hardwood heel. **bottom** Two views of a black and aubergine leather court shoe featuring the designer's signature set-in heel made from striped Brazilian hardwoods. The upper also features a contrasting sculptural leather detail.

40

Opposite White ankle boot. See p. 45 for details.
This page, top Two views of a chocolate-brown and coffee leather ankle boot with fold-down top line and striped Brazilian hardwood heel.
bottom A pair of white T-strap court shoes with a set-in hardwood heel.

'Shoes are the right combination of fashion and architecture.'

Julia Lundsten

Opposite and page 42 Elaborate white ankle boot with a sharply pointed toe and hardwood heel. The upper is formed from a pleated side quarter with a bronze ridged-leather trim and has a serrated top line.

This page Side and rear view of a black leather ankle boot with a pointed toe and wooden heel. The upper has a raw-edged ridged bronze leather trim and raw-edged top line.

45

bruno frisoni

Despite having Italian parents, designer Bruno Frisoni is a true Parisian. Born in France in 1960, he began his career working for legendary designers Jean-Louis Scherrer, Maryll Lanvin and Christian Lacroix. He went on to work freelance as a consultant for the houses of Trussardi, Givenchy and Yves Saint Laurent Rive Gauche. This experience led to an exceptional breadth and depth of couture design knowledge and nurtured his taste for 'haute fantasy' footwear.

In 1999 Frisoni launched his own shoe collection, although this was not always his intention. 'When I started working, I wanted to design clothes, but I soon developed a passion for accessories, especially for shoes because although you just carry a bag with you, a shoe actually becomes a part of you.' Even now, Frisoni works straight from the body, draping fabric and ribbons on the feet like a true couturier.

Decidedly more decorative than minimalist, his creations feature interlaced leather and fabric and are adorned with creative trims, such as beading and buckles. 'I'm not into pure design,' he says, 'as the technical aspect of the shoe is not really that interesting to me.' He prefers to concern himself with the decoration as 'the structure doesn't count that much, it is the intention that is behind it that is essential.' Therefore, the first step Frisoni takes before designing a shoe is to outline a silhouette and create an attitude. 'I always start from a silhouette that projects the allure I am looking for,' he says, and 'from there I arrive at a shape, then work on the forceful contours that will eventually define my collection.'

As well as designing his own line, Frisoni was appointed artistic director of Roger Vivier in 2004. In taking control of the world-renowned brand, Frisoni has mined the rich artistic heritage of the 'stiletto King', cleverly reinterpreting the innovative cheekiness of the Vivier style. Frisoni draws his creative inspiration from the richness of the Vivier brand while simultaneously allowing himself the liberty to vary and reinterpret it.

This is of course an important appointment for Frisoni, as Roger Vivier has been famously credited with transforming footwear history. Vivier's landmark designs include the first stiletto heel, created in 1954, named after a type of knife, and which accentuates the curve of the leg; the comma heel, created in 1963, which curls in like a reverse comma, dramatically arching the foot; and the square-toed flats worn by Catherine Deneuve in the 1965 film *Belle du Jour*. Charged with the responsibility of updating these signature shapes for the twenty-first century, Frisoni injects the Vivier brand with youthful energy and flashy acid brights. When designing the Roger Vivier collections, Frisoni says he simply digs into his memory because 'in my view, this isn't a reissue; it's a reinterpretation.'

Opposite Velvet and satin stiletto. See p. 49 for details.

'I'm not into pure design.'

Bruno Frisoni

Opposite, top left Design sketch for a cigarette-heel peep-toe court shoe with front ribbon detail. **top right** Sketch of a low-heeled ballerina with decorative tongue detail. **bottom left** Design for a forepart platform sandal with high chunky heel and oversized ribbon and bow details. **bottom right** Original sketch for a black stiletto-heel sandal with oversized ribbon bow detail and brass rivets.

This page, top Denim-jacket court shoe with an unbuttoned vamp and flash highlight of a red inner heel. **bottom** Sensual red velvet and black satin 115mm-stiletto sandal with forepart platform and oversized bow detail.

Unquestionably feminine, this 100mm-stiletto-heel ankle-strap sandal has a cut-away upper and moulded yellow gold quarter panels.

pierre hardy

Pierre Hardy is unquestionably one of luxury footwear's leading luminaries, having spent over twenty years at the helm of some of France's most prestigious fashion houses before launching his self-titled label in 1998 to critical acclaim. The basis of Hardy's style could perhaps be described as modern simplicity. 'I try to simplify the design to an essence,' he explains. 'I love clean lines and sculptural shapes and I try to make shoes as powerful, clear and sensual as possible.' Indeed, his bold, statuesque forms stand proud; they are works of art in their own right, exuding a pronounced sex appeal.

His ability to create these simple silhouettes is dependent on his decision to avoid mixing materials. Instead, he often uses a material in its entirety so as not to distract the eye from the form of the shoe itself. 'I always try to choose one material, not several, such as plain metal, plain wood and patent. I am not really into mixing and combining many materials with too many details.'

Hardy says that he 'strives to express femininity, but in an ambiguous way, mixing it with strength or masculinity, or sometimes with a more provocative mood.' Maintaining his position at the pinnacle of modernity is something he is extremely passionate about, explaining 'I always try to bring something new in the most radical way I can'.

When creating a concept, Hardy does not work by any predefined methods, rather more by chance, his influences often far ranging and unrelated to fashion. 'The way I work is really abstract; I almost disconnect with reality in the beginning. My inspiration comes from very different things that look beautiful to me. It can be objects, places, art, but never a character or a fantasy story.' Regardless of the source of inspiration, however, the concept always starts with

a sketch: 'The initial step is always a drawing, first because most of my ideas come from drawing. Second, if I have an idea in mind, I try to give it shape in the drawing.'

While studying fine arts and painting, Hardy would frequently sketch shoe ideas in his spare time, and then a chance career opportunity arose at Dior in 1988. As he recalls, 'It was suggested to me as an illustrator to work on the shoe collection'. After five years at Dior, Hardy went on to become the head of design at Hermès and then head designer for Balenciaga footwear in 2000, and he is still in residence at both.

Simultaneously working for three very different brands requires a measured approach and his design process varies greatly, depending on the brand for which he is creating. 'Alternating between Hermès, Balenciaga and my own collection is like acting out different characters in three different scripts. My own collection is very much a one-man show, Hermès is a big-budget production, while Balenciaga is an art-house film.'

Opposite Silver and black ankle boots. See p. 56 for details.

'I love clean lines and sculptural shapes.' Pierre Hardy

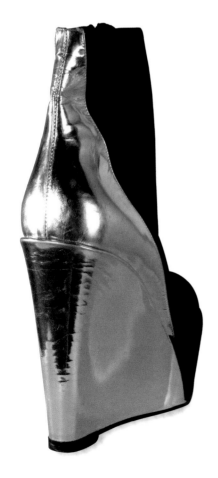

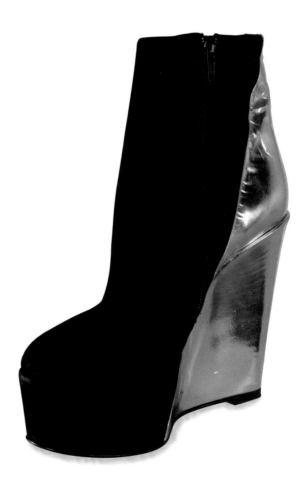

Page 54 and page 55, top Gold wedge sandals with covered ridged wedge, asymmetric fanned multi-strap uppers and ankle-strap fastenings.
Page 55, bottom This silver and black suede and leather platform wedge ankle boot evokes the mood of Ziggy Stardust.
This page, top Inky-blue suede and bronze wedge sandal with two-part caged upper and double ankle-strap fastenings. **bottom and overleaf** Vibrant jade-green suede and glacé kid striped wedge sandal with ankle fastening and peep toe.

This page, top left Gold leather and flesh-coloured suede shoe with stiletto heel and double ankle-strap fastening. **bottom left** Black suede stiletto-heel peep-toe court shoe with a frivolous polka-dot lace ankle trim.

right from top Design sketch of an open-toed shoe with ankle-strap fastening and wedge heel; sketch of a stiletto-heel, pointed-toe court shoe; design for a court shoe with forepart platform in a bold lined material; strong graphic silhouette of a two-tone chunky-heel shoe.

guillaume hinfray

An historian at heart, French designer Guillaume Hinfray looks no further than his Norman heritage for inspiration for his work. 'Season after season I am travelling through the different ages and places of the history of my region: Normandy,' he says. 'I am fascinated by the history of the Vikings too, and follow them from the fjords to Normandy and Britain, from Sicily to Byzantium.'

Combining this knowledge of history and costume with his study of fascinating and, at times, seemingly futuristic details of armour, harnesses and chain-mail, Hinfray aims to strike a balance between the rough and the elegant. An example of this is in his use of studding: 'I like to add it to very plain styles to create disturbing elements in the traditionally luxurious world of fashion.'

Especially precious to Hinfray are the hidden parts of his shoes, with their sensual silk-satin linings and quilted inner soles. The uppers speak of sophistication and opulence in their use of satin bows, plissé, draping and sumptuous embroideries in such materials as velvety suede, kid, soft skin, kangaroo and devoré velvet. Hardware also recalls the past with oxidized brass or dark nickel buckles on flats and pumps.

Launched in Autumn/Winter 2003/04, Hinfray's first collection was dedicated to the great female warrior Joan of Arc, in which she was cast as a modern legend. His own revolutionary approach to footwear has also led to consultancy work for Bottega Veneta, Salvatore Ferragamo, Sergio Rossi (see p. 140) and L'Autre Chose.

Hinfray's background in fashion is impeccable, for after graduating from the esteemed Ecole de la Chambre Syndicale de la Couture in Paris, he gained experience working on haute couture for Rochas, Hermès and Lanvin.

This background in haute couture means that he is particularly keen on craftsmanship and attention to detail, and explains his belief that the inside of a shoe is just as important as the upper.

Hinfray fell into footwear design after working with his partner Marco Censi (see p. 16) on a book of shoes. Hinfray believes that the period when he started designing shoes was the golden age, when 'shoes for women stopped being only black, heeled pumps and became central to each woman's wardrobe.' Together the pair worked as consultants for several prêt-a-porter labels and, in 2000, they founded their first footwear brand, Amaterasu, with its strongly innovative yet refined character.

The aesthetic melting pot of the Guillaume Hinfray collection, however, always returns to the theme of his Norman descent and the marriage of these ancestors with a 'street-culture' nature. Indeed, his own legacy has certain parallels with the culture of his much-admired Vikings. Both have been capable of assimilating the various cultures of the areas they encounter, from Graeco-Roman to Arab, generating a new sort of cultural democracy. All of this is revealed in Hinfray's tastes, which translate into a 'neo-global' aesthetic.

Opposite Platform sandal. See p. 62 for details.

This page, top Attention-grabbing peep-toe platform sandal in textured metallic leather with bronze ornamental hardware and an ankle-strap fastening. bottom Flesh-pink suede open court shoe with a decorative heel cup and an ankle-strap fastening. The raw-edged leather appliqué is trimmed with a faceted ruby-red stone. Opposite Sketch for a stacked-leather-heel peep-toe court shoe with intricate cut-outs and metal-ring hardware.

'Season after season I travel through the history of my region.' Guillaume Hinfray

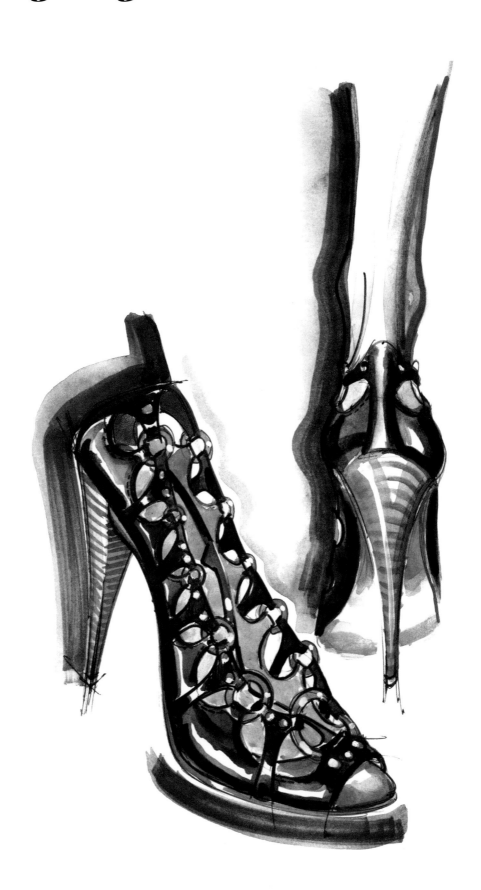

Hot metallic-red pointed-toe court shoe with a stiletto heel and decorative cut-out top line.

Pirate-inspired knee-high leather boot with chartreuse satin lining and knotted leather ankle-tie trim.

Over-the-knee flesh-coloured leather boot
with ruby-red satin lining and chocolate-brown
knotted tassel trim.

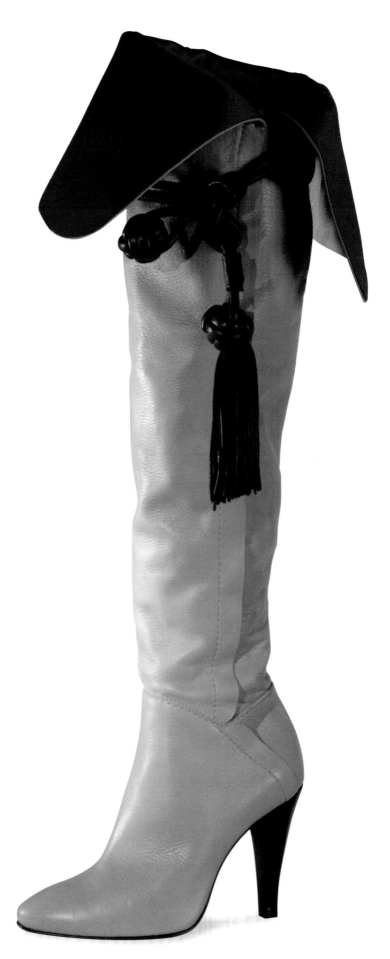

jenne o

Not for the faint-hearted, Jennefer Osterhoudt's shoes mix luxury skins with bold colours and extreme shapes for a strong and fetishistic look. Her collections comprise elegant and luxurious shoes and boots, inspired by the tall, round-toed, fetish boots of 1950s cabaret and striptease, and referencing lingerie and corsetry techniques. 'What sets me apart is the sexiness and the sensuality of my designs. I'm not ashamed of that. In fact, I celebrate it,' she declares.

Originally from Mission, a predominantly Spanish district of San Francisco, Osterhoudt studied Costume Design at Parsons School of Design in New York. Upon completion of her final year in Paris, she accepted an internship with John Galliano, which resulted in a permanent position as his chief accessories designer and thus her inauguration into footwear design. She finally launched her own distinctive line of elegant, fetish-inspired footwear in 2003.

Osterhoudt's former forays into costume design have clearly left a lasting impression on her, for while her shoes are elegant they also possess a dark, theatrical attitude. She is heavily inspired by the theatre of footwear as her designs reference 'American trailer culture, rock stars, 50s pin-ups and burlesque performers'. Perhaps uniquely, Osterhoudt also admits to keeping a collection of photographs of old ladies wearing orthopaedic shoes on her mobile phone.

It is this assimilation of such a range of influences that really marks Osterhoudt's style. She readily accepts that she has been inspired by nearly every youth subculture of the past forty years – citing mod, punk, glam, new romantic, Goth, rock and the New York club culture of the early 1990s.

The designer's sultry style cleverly balances sophistication with the more sinister side of sexuality; flesh tones, pinks and nudes make up her signature colours, while lingerie techniques are evident in the oversized silk bows and corsetry-style lacing of her shoes and boots. 'I like my shoes to have a strong girly sexiness to them,' she says. 'I love high stiletto heels combined with a short and fetishistic, round toe shape.' Materials and colour are very important; Osterhoudt uses the most luxurious reptile and lambskin leathers available, then mixes dusty neutrals with bright colours and metallics to create a variety of textures and tones in a single design.

She refuses to bow to commercial aspects of current trends, believing that 'due to the current economic climate, a lot of designers are playing it safe'. A backlash to this tendency towards safety is inevitable, and Osterhoudt is at the forefront of the new breed of designers who are pushing the boundaries in terms of design and the technologies of construction.

For an up-and-coming shoe designer, Osterhoudt already boasts an impressive cv. Over the past decade she has not only worked as head of accessories for the fashion houses of John Galliano, Givenchy and Alexander McQueen, but has also collaborated with footwear legends Manolo Blahník and Christian Louboutin. More recently, she has acted as a consultant for designers Raphael Lopez, Gharani Strok and Chloé. Working with such an array of talent has inevitably inspired her to expand her work. She has plans for a bag range, jewelry collection and maybe even hosiery sets: 'I want a whole Jenne O brand!' she exclaims.

Opposite 'Sarah I' is a metallic and matt lambskin court shoe in mushroom with a neon orange toe piece and a 100mm stiletto heel.

Previous spread Named after the female guitarist of rockabilly band The Cramps, 'Poison I', shown here in coral lambskin, is a double-sided lace-up ankle boot with a 100mm, 1970s-style chunky heel and short round toe.
This page An elegant strappy sandal with a 100mm stiletto heel and short round toe, designed for fashion designer Jean-Pierre Braganza.

This page Inspired by Iggy Pop's famous trousers, 'Iggy P', shown here as a sketch and in silver and navy lambskin, is an ankle-skimming boot with a 100mm heel, ruched elastic tongue and short round toe.
Overleaf and page 75, top Named after burlesque performer Dita von Teese, 'Dita V' is a ballet-slipper-inspired ankle boot. In flesh-pink snakeskin and lambskin, the style has a 100mm stiletto heel, short round toe shape and flesh-coloured satin bow, which ties at the ankle like a ballet slipper.
Page 75, bottom 'Farah F', so-called after Farah Fawcett, is a peep-toe sandal with a 100mm stiletto heel and short round last shape. Neon orange is complemented by bronze lambskin and the bronze silk bow is not only a decorative detail but also has a functional purpose as it adjusts the fit across the toes.

'My designs reference American trailer culture, 50s pin-ups and burlesque performers.' Jennefer Osterhoudt

max
kibardin

Siberian-born Max Kibardin is relatively new to the footwear world, having started his own brand in 2004. Kibardin's approach to design combines feminine elegance with structural engineering; a style influenced by his background in architecture and later cemented by his fashion design studies at the Istituto Marangoni in Milan.

Pioneering Kibardin's style is not easy, especially as he strives for a minimalist approach. 'Simplicity is a difficult mission in the beginning as you have to get noticed,' he says, 'and it is always the more whimsical designers who catch the attention of the press.'

Kibardin combines streamlined silhouettes with intricate architectural layers, brushed metallic heels and curvaceous wedges that are reminiscent of Art Deco columns. This method of design relies heavily on maintaining objectivity, an approach he perfected during his architectural training and one that ensures that the form of the shoe precedes colour and fabrication. 'Rarely do I conduct colour and fabric research before designing,' he says. 'In fact, normally I am searching for the fabrics with finished drawings in my hand.' Attention to detail is paramount for Kibardin and his shoes are painstakingly handcrafted from over fifty different processes, taking up to three weeks to produce.

Like all good architects, Kibardin begins with the foundations. A fascination with Mother Nature encourages him to re-create architectural blueprints of vegetal structures to form the integral framework of his shoes. As for fabrication, although Kibardin is particularly fond of exotic skins, he opts for simpler materials that accentuate his cleverly constructed creations. Regarding colour, he looks to exotic minerals and gemstones for inspiration.

Preparation for a collection starts several months before the design process begins. Immersing himself in his archive of movies, old magazines, art, nature and architecture, Kibardin considers his interests and the things he loves, and 'one day it all comes together like a piece of mosaic'. He finds the past a great influence: 'I love the femininity of the 1950s, the minimal elegance of the 1960s, and the colour and the pattern play of the 1970s.' His favourite Kibardin collection was inspired by Jacqueline Kennedy wearing her preferred designer Oleg Cassini, with prints influenced by the paintings of Mark Rothko.

At an early age, Kibardin drew what he calls 'the beauty in the everyday', a practice that helped him escape the uniformity of soviet reality and enabled him to develop his style. His interest in shoes was first ignited in 2002 by a conversation with Fabio Zambernardi, design director at Prada and Miu Miu, while showing Zambernardi his own prêt-a-porter womenswear collection: 'Suddenly I was asked if I was interested in shoes. Even if I wasn't initially, I started to think about it,' Kibardin recalls.

Opposite 'Samantha' court shoe. See p. 78 for details.

This page, top Aubergine peep-toe 'Samantha' court shoe with hand-stitched linear quilting and 100mm-high bronze lamé leather-covered heel. **bottom** Demi-wedge version of the 'Samantha' court shoe pictured above.

Grey 'Nina' ankle boot with contrasting lizard heel and strap fastening.

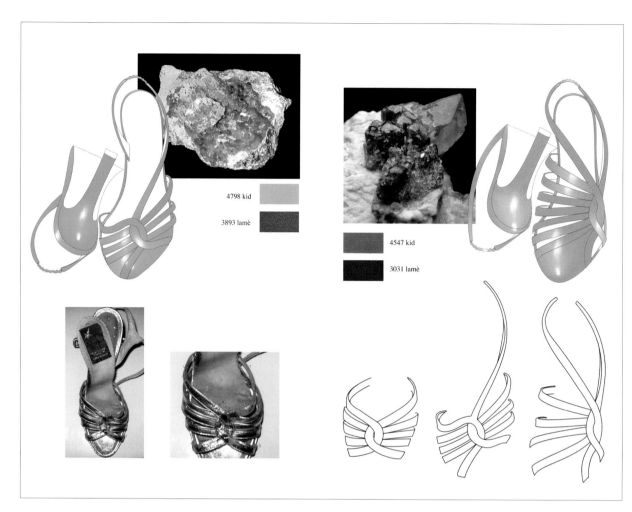

4798 kid

3893 lamè

4547 kid

3031 lamè

combination of bordeaux with soft pink(suede)("funny face"1956)

important presence of bordeaux
(110mm patent leather wedge)

389 suede

383 patent leather

toe detail,
double stitching

Opposite Initial design sketches and inspiration for Kibardin's Spring/Summer 2006 collection. **This page** Pretty peach and cherry-red 'Catherine' shoe with a 110mm patent-leather-covered wedge heel. The soft kid suede and patent leather combination is cut at the vamp to reveal toe cleavage.

Overleaf and page 83, left Cherry-red 'Madlene' ankle boot in soft kid suede. This dramatic shape was created with a 100mm stiletto heel, almond toe and cut out upper and heel upper. Kibardin then added sculptural layers inspired by the form of artichokes to the outer ankle.
Page 83, right Red suede 'Séverine' ankle boot with a layered sculptural toe and a cut-away heel upper with a contrasting black elastic insert.

'One day it all comes together like a piece of mosaic.' Max Kibardin

nicholas
kirkwood

From sculptural, crescent uppers and rhombus-shaped heels, to chevron-patterned, stacked-leather heels and aluminium-plate fastenings, Nicholas Kirkwood's shoes have one common theme: they are evidence of a master craftsman at work.

Despite the hints of modernist architecture and sculpture in his footwear, Kirkwood denies taking inspiration from anything so specific. 'I doodle a lot and let my designs evolve quite freely,' he admits. 'I rarely set out thinking, "this is what I am going to do", and, in fact, the only thing I ever try and do is test out new ideas.' He does, however, consider good design to be work that is modern and pushes the boundaries, such as Le Corbusier's Villa Savoye near Paris, which embraces clean, flat lines and juxtaposes materials to create a modern aesthetic.

Strict linear composition devoid of clutter is clearly central to his aesthetic. He rejects fussy trims, bows and diamantés, describing them as 'the gargoyles of the footwear world', and dismisses stilettos for being 'too old-fashioned'. Instead, Kirkwood chooses to rely on colour and materials to emphasize the graphic constructions of his work.

'It's all about the silhouettes….It's about the shape of the last and about the shape of the actual pattern that's drawn on to the last, and colour or material combinations. I don't use anything that's stuck on to the shoe. In certain ways it's architectural. Old-fashioned buildings like to be very decorative on the outside, but the basic shape is still a block, whereas modern buildings are more concerned about the actual shape of the building itself, rather than what's put on as ornamentation. That's sort of the way I try to think of my shoes, especially when it comes to the heels.'

Kirkwood launched his eponymous line in 2005, aged just twenty-four, following a five-year apprenticeship with Britain's most well-known milliner, Philip Treacy, and a period of study at Cordwainers College, London. While never tempted to become a hat designer himself, Kirkwood says shoes and hats share something in common: 'They must fit and fulfil a practical purpose'.

With typical pioneering resolve, Kirkwood avoids using any fastenings in his collections, choosing instead to challenge his materials – stingray, lizard and ostrich skin, and butter-soft nappa leather. He folds the materials like origami, twisting them to explore their possibilities. The results are beautiful pieces of footwear, where stripped-back stingray skin resembles stained glass and uppers make grand sculptural statements.

Since launching his own collection, Kirkwood has also collaborated with several other fashion labels including John Rocha, Frost French, Boudicca and Ashley Isham. In addition, he hopes to launch a men's line in the future to further his groundbreaking style.

Opposite Candy-pink 'Arp' sandal inspired by the sculptures of Jean Arp. The sandal has an architectural circular upper, a chevron stacked pink-and-white leather veneer heel and a floating instep closure.

'It's all about the silhouettes.'

Nicholas Kirkwood

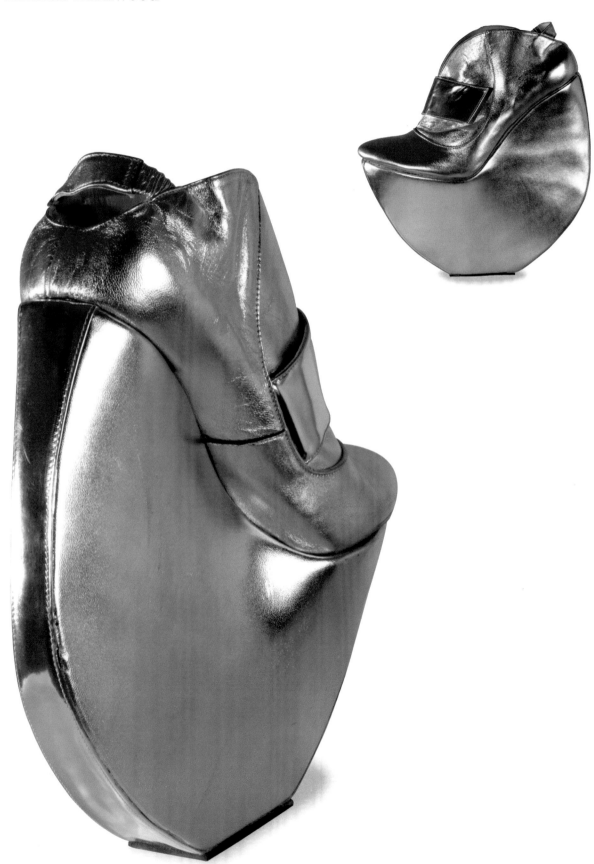

Opposite Gold circular platform shoe that highlights Kirkwood's sculptural aesthetic.
This page, top 'Revealer' is a coral-coloured kid and shaved stingray court shoe with a 105mm chevron stacked pink-and-white veneer conical heel and a rounded toe.
middle Black kid nappa ankle-bound T-strap shoe with a 105mm stacked-leather veneer conical heel with a continuous upper heel façade. **bottom** Black leather and fur ankle bootie with front buckle detail.

Previous spread and opposite 'Barbarella' is a T-strap open court shoe made for Jean-Pierre Braganza's Spring/Summer 2006 catwalk show. Crafted from perforated calf, the shoe features a 105mm chromed conical heel and low-curved floating aluminium strap riveted on to the shoe.

This page, top left Sketch for a black kid and shaved-stingray-skin sling back with a circular cut-out on the upper and a 105mm tapered square back heel in wood. **middle left** Design for a python instep sandal with sculptural milled aluminium toe post and a 100mm aluminium pierced heel. **bottom left** Sketch for a black kid nappa ankle-bound T-strap shoe with a 105mm stacked-leather veneer conical heel with a continuous upper heel façade. **right** Original design for a kid nappa and shaved-stingray boot with stacked-leather veneer conical heel and rounded toe. The boot has a ruched leather back with toggle detailing that cleverly reveals a stingray underside.

laetitia's

Feminine and sensual, Leticia Lara Vella's brand Laetitia'S has successfully cultivated its own niche in the footwear market through the use of a unique last shape. The brand's signature silhouette protrudes gently at the front, emphasizing the shape of the toe. This simple yet unexpected shape is used to underpin Laetitia'S entire collection and is inspired by the natural curves of the foot.

The brand was originally created out of sheer exasperation because Vella continually found herself trying to squeeze her four inches of foot into the one-inch space of a typical pointed toe. She was compelled to find a new solution that would create less restrictive shoes, which were still sexy yet eliminated agony and poor posture. By avoiding less forgiving last shapes, Vella's footwear offers genuine comfort and practicality to the wearer while also commanding attention for its stylish silhouettes and use of materials.

With the signature last shape remaining largely unchanged each season, Vella has more time to concentrate on fine-tuning the most intricate details of footwear design, such as heel heights and uppers, elements that must develop and adapt to the changing seasonal trends. Taking her cue from footwear design legends Roger Vivier, Salvatore Ferragamo and Manolo Blahník, Vella also enjoys embellishment, creating mosaics of exquisite Venetian Murano glass buttons, nacre (mother-of-pearl) and natural shell, imitation ivory and silk ribbons for her footwear. Invariably, she is happy to work solely with leather as a base material, occasionally introducing exotic skins such as python, lizard and ostrich to create texture and surface interest, or employing luminescent metallics or arresting print designs for visual stimulation.

Content in her habitual surroundings, Vella is inspired by the everyday, basing entire design concepts, colour and material choices on chance happenings however memorable or mundane. 'I find inspiration in everything; a song, a movie, a landscape, even a conversation, it all depends on the mood or the moment.'

Having never studied footwear design, Vella is in the enviable position of being able to approach her designs without being swayed by preconceived notions or ideas. Originally trained as a film technician and set decorator, she discovered her true calling when a chance opportunity to design a small collection of limited-edition ballerina pumps eventually led her into footwear design.

Launching her own brand, Laetitia'S, in 2003, Vella clearly remains focused on the footwear industry. However, she does not rule out future expansions into new areas of design and, regardless of her current success, she is only too aware of how difficult it can be to create a luxury label in today's unpredictable market. She remains positive however, declaring, 'I am happy to be selling my shoes all over the world, without losing my spirit, even if they are only small collections.'

Opposite Silver printed-leather stiletto court shoe. See p. 94 for details.

This page, top Sophisticated silver printed-leather stiletto court shoe with a low-cut vamp. The shoe features Laetitia'S signature last shape, which follows the natural form of the foot. **bottom** Brown leather cut-away court shoe with contrasting coral lizard-skin asymmetric upper.

Opposite Citrus-yellow stiletto-heel sandal featuring Laetitia'S signature last toe shape, a scalloped-edge toe strap and tangerine-orange satin ribbon ankle tie.

94

This page Working drawings illustrating
Laetitia'S range building.
Opposite, top Playful pink kitten-heel court
shoe with asymmetric top line and polka-dot
ribbon ankle tie. The suede is printed with
a dot transfer and the design also incorporates
nacre hardware and a silver leather lining.
bottom Flat cream leather sandal with a ruched
silver leather trim and glass-and-wooden
button-bead hardware.

'I find inspiration in everything.'

Leticia Lara Vella

Chocolate-brown stiletto-heel court shoe with
Bordeaux-red, chocolate-brown and moss-green
velvet ribbon stripes.

ld tuttle

As a professional ballet dancer, Tiffany Tuttle has always had an inherent fascination with the physical beauty of the foot. 'I love looking at and focusing on the three-dimensional shape of a shoe,' she says, 'particularly as it becomes something completely new when worn.'

Like many American designers, Tuttle started her design career as a student at the Fashion Institute of Technology in New York, before continuing her studies at Milan's Ars Arpel Academy for Footwear Design. She established her brand LD Tuttle in 2004 with her husband and partner LD, a print designer and technical illustrator. She now divides her time between Italy, where her shoes are produced, and her home in Los Angeles.

Strangely drawn to details that are incongruous or create friction within their environment, Tuttle finds something particularly appealing about her hometown of Los Angeles. 'With its gritty urban life and scenic landscapes, it's kind of ugly but at the same time very beautiful.' The synergy of these natural and artificial influences is the springboard for her design aesthetic. 'It's the dynamic change caused when these elements meet that I find so intriguing. Often things that I find beautiful are simply things that I'm just not used to,' Tuttle explains.

She is influenced by such reality as well as by elements frequently unrelated to footwear, such as photographs by Diane Arbus or the exposed angular subjects of Egon Schiele's paintings. However, Tuttle's true inspiration comes from sources that are somewhat more oblique, fusing her reality with fantasy and literature. Whether it is 'mythical sea monsters, ancient shipwrecks or forgotten caves' and the worlds she finds there, these elements often weave their way into her collections.

A self-confessed history buff, Tuttle has always been fascinated by primary sources and she enjoys the challenge of translating her raw creative ideas into finished products. 'With each design phase, I try to strip away the extraneous and inject something vital or more specific,' she says. 'Ideally, each idea conveys an emotion – that way you know you are hitting something that is real and that women will identify with.' She begins designing with a general silhouette, which dictates the last she uses, the heel and the shape of the shoe.

Her collections combine modern silhouettes and intriguing design contrasts, a winning formula that appeals to a self-assured female audience. Using functional hardware in a decorative capacity, she cleverly creates a strong sexy attitude with a hint of utilitarian-style glamour. Tuttle's love of contrast also informs her pioneering use of fabrics and textures. She employs an unorthodox approach to material mixing, where robust natural-grain leathers with synthetic high-gloss finishes meet delicate tulle woven with sturdy metal chain.

Her high-heel décolleté style from the Autumn/Winter 06 collection features a large loop of leather suggesting an oversized bow, which comes up to the arch of the foot. This loop creates a shape away from the foot that is striking in itself and at the same time highlights the delicate nature of the arch of the foot. Tuttle's incongruous aesthetic similarly inspires her use of colour, offsetting predominately neutral tones with vibrant bursts of clashing brights: 'I think that the collections convey a feeling of organic punk,' she concludes.

Opposite Mustard-seed 'Quasimodo' sandal. See p. 102 for details.

This page Quilted T-strap 'Quasimodo' sandal with a 90mm stacked cone heel. Quilted bumps of amorphous satin contrast beautifully with the contrapunto stitching on the leather upper.
Opposite, top 'Phenix' sling-back sandal and sketch with a 90mm stacked cone heel and rounded last shape. The upper is decorated with a rope of braided cotton tulle and gunmetal chain. **middle** Striking black calfskin 'Grendel' court shoe and sketch with a 90mm stacked cone heel, pointed toe and oversized tongue.
bottom Black 'Umbra' peep-toe court shoe with amorphous satin quilting and a stacked cone heel.

'Ideally, each idea conveys an emotion.'

Tiffany Tuttle

Opposite and this page, bottom 'Medusa' is a petrol ostrich-stamped velvet peep-toe sling back with a 90mm stacked cone heel, decorative suede fringing and a zipper down the vamp.
This page, top Nubuck, natural-grain leather and patent sling-back sandal with an oversized tongue and chunky stacked-leather heel.

Overleaf Black calfskin 'Grendel' court shoe with a 90mm stacked cone heel, pointed toe and oversized tongue.

benoît
méléard

Manolo Blahník recently declared that Benoît Méléard is one of the most important footwear designers of his generation. Coming from perhaps the most highly regarded shoe designer of our time, this grand statement commands us to sit up and take notice.

No stranger to the headlines now, Méléard became known in the mid-1990s when he began developing radical footwear for Alexander McQueen, Hussein Chalayan and Jeremy Scott. For Scott, he created a much publicized, and subsequently much imitated, cloven-hoof pump, which cemented his reputation as a footwear visionary.

In 1998, Méléard launched his own line of shoes with a catwalk show in Paris, becoming the first designer in the city to create such a show purely for shoes. Just three years after launching his footwear label, Méléard was chosen for the prestigious Best Designer for the City of Paris award – the first time that the accolade had been bestowed upon a shoe designer.

The beauty of Méléard's work lies in his refusal to compromise his artistic integrity. He often designs bizarre and aesthetically absurd footwear yet he also manages to satisfy the needs of a commercial market. This ability was cleverly employed in his recent collection, created for London fashion designer Gareth Pugh's Spring/Summer 2007 catwalk show.

Méléard is a great inspiration not only in his use of colour and shape, but also in the way that he challenges our very expectations of footwear. Common to all his collections are pronounced geometric themes – from the strong lines of his first collection, called 'Cruel', to his collection 'O', which is based on the shape of a circle

and influenced by the iconic fashion designer and performance artist, the late Leigh Bowery.

The designs may have an uncompromising appearance, but Méléard insists that they are not only wearable but comfortable. His hands-on approach – his collections are entirely handcrafted – is the result of an ongoing passion, and he works with people who are also dedicated to their craft. 'If it doesn't work at first, you try again and again until it does,' he says, 'You don't learn your job sitting in a studio. You learn it in the factory. It may not be glamorous, but you have to get your technical experience first.'

This philosophy has won Méléard the approval of his contemporaries and the establishment, and his work is exhibited in several museums around the world, including the Louvre in Paris.

Opposite Black and red diagonally striped leather shoe from the 'Tip Toe' collection in 1998. The shoe has a box toe and industrial nut-and-bolt steel heel. The oversized decorative tongue folds indulgently over the toe.

Black leather heel-less shoe with a box toe
and oversize button detailing.

Black and red leather heel-less shoe with a box toe. Upward-fanning leather from the toe adds further drama to the theatrical shape.

This page Original sketches by Benoît Méléard, 2005, in cooperation with French artist Claude Lévêque, and first seen in the graphics installation 'D-Evian' by Bertrand Allombert.
Opposite Black suede stiletto-heel court shoe with moulded almond toe shape mounted on an extended pointed last shape. Circles of ivy-green satin and Méléard's signature ribbon heel tab emphasize the shoe's sculptural quality.

112

'If it doesn't work at first, you try again and again.'

Benoît Méléard

Opposite This crazy shoe formed part of Méléard's 1999 'O' collection, which was created as a tribute to Leigh Bowery and Patrick Kelly. The shoe incorporates a box toe, industrial nut-and-bolt heel and an oversized appliqué leather button.
This page From the same collection is this white and turquoise spotted-leather box-toe boot with no heel.

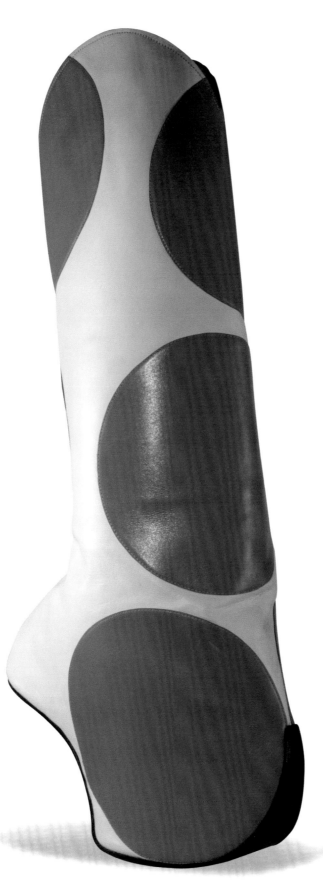

chie mihara

In a style she describes as 'romantic and naïve', Chie Mihara employs many of the techniques and constructions of an authentic master craftsman, creating hand-sculpted last shapes with toes and heels from the finest natural skins. She creates her shoes with quality, comfort and design in mind, crafting fine-quality footwear that is a joy to wear.

In keeping with this artisanal approach, Mihara works exclusively with leather, skilfully manipulating, plaiting, pleating and ruching raw-edged vegetable tan leathers to create beautiful and sculptural upper designs. Such is her love for leather that she also rejects using standard metal hardware for accessories, opting instead to create her own shoe ornaments, such as scalloped fringing and oriental knots, from the leftover scraps of skins.

Colour also plays a pivotal role in Mihara's designs and she goes to extreme measures to ensure that she can work with the exact shades of deep blackcurrant, mint green or mustard that her shoes require. Each season the designer painstakingly develops her own leather dyes and colours, which become the foundation for each new collection and lend her footwear their unique quality.

Comfort is paramount to Mihara's philosophy and she happily insists on using an anatomical footbed in each design. 'I want my shoes to be beautiful and beauty must also be comfortable,' she says.

While Mihara undoubtedly adheres to the prescribed rhythm of the seasons, she chooses always to lead with her signature style: 'I don't follow any particular fashion trends, although I do consider myself to have popular taste.' Her collections frequently reference footwear history – alluding to the definitive shoes of the 1920s, 1930s and 1950s – and feature styles that are both feminine and avant-garde, such as upturned toes and sculptural heel shapes.

Born in Brazil to Japanese parents, Mihara first began her design career as a teenager, selling design sketches to a Brazilian dress manufacturer, before moving to Japan to work for apparel designer Junko Koshino. Disillusioned by the fashion industry, she spent six months in New York practising sculpture. However, 'six months sculpting and I realized I needed fashion back in my life,' she recalls. 'I thought about what the resulting combination of sculpture and fashion would be and my answer was shoes.'

After first studying accessories at the Fashion Institute of Technology in New York, Mihara moved to Spain in 1995 to design for Charles Jourdan. She then launched her own label in 2001, supported by her husband, a footwear factory owner. Despite concerns about the current shift towards mass-production within the footwear industry, Mihara remains optimistic. 'I hope the culture of quality shoemaking doesn't disappear,' she says, 'I think it can, and will, survive with the manufacture of even more exclusive and specialized designer shoes.'

Opposite Polished nappa Mary Jane. See p. 119 for details.

'I want my shoes to be beautiful and comfortable.'

Chie Mihara

Opposite, top Butter-soft nappa sandal in aqua with a 65mm cone-shaped two-tone vertically stacked heel in brown and nude. Soft goatskin is woven into a decorative vamp with a Sam Browne stud fastening. **bottom** Tan sling-back pump featuring Mihara's signature domed toe shape with a saddle seam. This shoe is crafted from waxed goatskin with a 65mm two-tone vertically stacked heel and a decorative punched appliqué upper. The buckle fastening is painted and distressed, suggesting a lifetime of wear.

This page Polished nappa Mary Jane in aubergine with a round toe and 75mm heel. The scalloped-leather upper is layered like fish scales, while inside an anatomical footbed provides the ultimate in a comfortable heel. **Overleaf** Smoke-grey suede and nappa leather calf-high boot. Inspired by the mixing of geometric lines from the Art Deco period, the boot has a domed toe shape and a 75mm stacked heel.

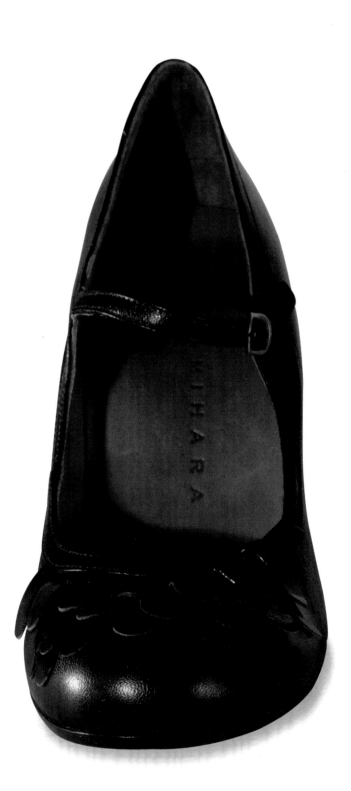

Original sketch for the teal sandal, pictured below, which is made from soft grainy nappa leather with a two-tone vertically stacked wedge heel.

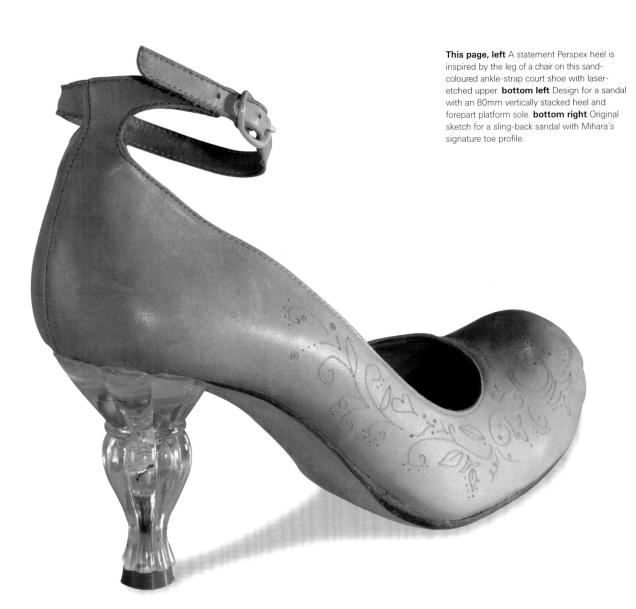

This page, left A statement Perspex heel is inspired by the leg of a chair on this sand-coloured ankle-strap court shoe with laser-etched upper. **bottom left** Design for a sandal with an 80mm vertically stacked heel and forepart platform sole. **bottom right** Original sketch for a sling-back sandal with Mihara's signature toe profile.

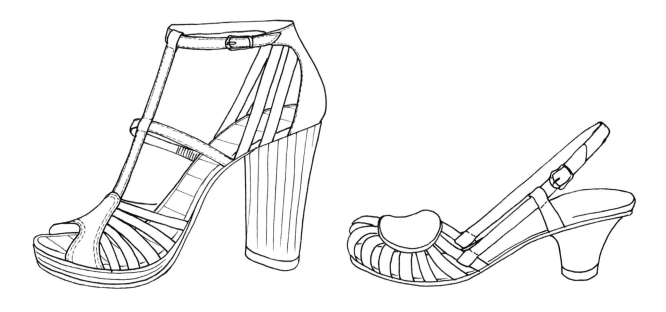

miharayasuhiro

Tokyo-based designer MIHARAYASUHIRO is renowned for his innovative footwear collections, most of which focus on experimentation with leather. His work stands out for its stripped down simplicity and fine craftsmanship. The designer explains, 'I don't set out to design fantasies. Over design is a weakness and, instead, I choose to concentrate on simple forms that enable the basic idea to emerge.'

The designer credits his eccentric upbringing for his creative ideas. Son of an abstract painter and a chicken researcher, he grew up in Fukuoka in the western part of Japan. Graduating from Tama Art University, Tokyo, in 1997, he went on to complete a short apprenticeship with a shoemaker, and immediately fell for the intricacies and techniques of the craft. He then taught himself the traditional methods of shoemaking, focusing on fine-quality craftsmanship and attention to detail. He progressed quickly; launching his own footwear line later in the same year and his first store, SOSU ('prime number') MIHARAYASUHIRO, in 1998. Since then he has been a familiar fixture on the Japanese fashion scene.

Like many Japanese designers, he works in a conceptual vein with great technical skill. His design philosophy is to break through the boundaries that have been built over the course of fashion history and to challenge our perceptions and stereotypes. He is interested in people's reaction to his creations and cites artist Marcel Duchamp's 'ready-mades' as a major influence. Above all, the designer seeks an emotive response. This is a design approach that he sums up perfectly: 'What you see is never what you get'.

'The one thing that struck me about leather shoemaking was the focus on authenticity and craftsmanship,' he explains. 'I wanted to use the same techniques but to bring them up to date with modern design.' The designer describes his work as 'the ridiculous meets the sublime', a theme that manifests itself in his signature raised-relief leather laces and boots lined with aluminium mesh.

It was this desire to create truly contemporary footwear that led him to design for sportswear company Puma. He was eager to study sneaker design, believing that it was a necessary step in his pursuit of a 'global knowledge of shoemaking'. 'Sneakers are entirely different from leather shoes,' he explains. 'They have no focus on authenticity; instead they are based on modern technologies and I thought that there was a possibility for some crossover between the two.' So, in 2000, inspired by people's obvious affection for their dirty old Pumas, he approached the company himself, offering to design a collection for them. The two have collaborated ever since, with each Puma Mihara collection allowing him to explore ever more diverse themes; for example, the Spring/Summer 04 collection emulated the way that muscles wrap around bones, using rubber pieces to envelop the whole shoe (including the sole) as a form of protection.

The designer remains pragmatic about his Puma range, explaining that 'the two lines, MIHARAYASUHIRO and Puma Mihara, are completely different. In terms of both purpose and achievement, my own line will always be the one that is closest to my heart.'

Opposite Black lace-up calfskin boot with a twisted toe shape. The upper of this shoe is stitched down but left loose, overhanging the sole.

Opposite Zip-up boot in brown calfskin featuring the designer's discreet signature raised-relief leather laces.
This page, right Design sketches illustrating range building. **bottom** Heavy-duty lace-up shoe in black creased leather.

'What you see is never what you get.'

MIHARAYASUHIRO

Opposite Green and caramel slip-on pigskin shoe with elastic inserts, contrasting coloured stitching and transparent membrane cover.
This page Zip-up ankle boot with a 17mm heel in bronze brushed calfskin and raised-relief leather laces.

Peep-toe pigskin court shoe with a transparent
membrane cover, revealing pearls and sequins
between the upper and the outer layer.

130

minna **parikka**

Magical swan wings, softly rounded toe shapes and curvaceous heels, Minna Parikka's shoes recall lavish imaginary worlds and captivate childlike hearts and adult minds alike. Although a relatively new addition to the footwear pantheon, Finnish-born Parikka has already secured herself a significant number of devotees, with her fairy-tale-edged femininity.

Parikka's shoes evoke a light-hearted sentiment, which alludes to fairy-tale fantasies and fictional romantic adventures, while referencing the definitive styles of the 1930s, 1940s and 1950s. 'It's all about the enjoyment of femininity and a time when women were elegant and wore matching accessories,' she explains. She considers her aesthetic playful yet feminine and believes having fun is very important, especially when designing. 'I want people to see that I have a good time when working on my collections,' she says. 'Inspiration comes from all of the good and bad experiences.'

Years of admiration for legendary shoe designers Salvatore Ferragamo and Roger Vivier have clearly had an impact on her style. Yet while her shoes are undoubtedly elegant, Parikka also references nostalgic childhood memories and 1950s-style pin-up girls. Above all, she is inspired by the things she loves most. 'I design for women who still have that little girl inside them who appreciates all those lovely girly things, regardless of their age.' She combines bold sculptural silhouettes with details from the delights of the gingerbread house and all its temptations. Heart-shaped cookie cut-outs and intricately embroidered swan wings complement exaggerated Louis heels trimmed with scalloped-edged fins to mimic the curvaceous contours of 1950s starlets.

When working with materials, Parikka has a leaning towards the less fussy options. 'I tend to use quite simple, basic materials because I want to concentrate more on the shapes and the details of the shoes. At the same time I like the contrast between shiny and matt surfaces within the same collection.' Creating subtle contrast is something Parikka is particularly fond of, mixing fuzzy suedes with highly polished patents and mouthwatering confectionery brights with ice-cream-coloured pastels.

Parikka studied Footwear Design at De Montfort University, Leicester, in the UK, before establishing her brand in 2005, although it was in her early teens that she first fell in love with the idea of being a shoe designer. 'Shoes are amazing objects that combine fashion and product design, both of which I find very interesting.' In the future, Parikka hopes to create a little romance, dreaming of being free to design beautiful shoes that women will fall in love with. 'I hope that more customers will demand more exciting products so that the industry keeps moving all the time, allowing more of the smaller brands like my own to push through.'

Opposite 'Sweetheart' lace-up boot. See p. 134 for details.

Black nubuck 'Edith' court shoe with a 30mm baroque heel and a rounded toe. The upper features a gold-embroidered leather wing detail, reinforced with iron wire to maintain the shape and to allow the wearer to adjust it according to her mood.

Opposite 'Sweetheart' lace-up ankle-skimming boot and sketches with a 70mm exaggerated Louis heel, trimmed with a scallop-edged fin. The boot is made from patent leather with an almond-shaped toe, white nappa trim and quirky heart-shaped lace ends.

134

135

With its rubber sole and pointed toe shape 'Teddina' is a girly twist on the brothel creeper. The upper is made from dusty lilac suede, which is trimmed with black patent running stitches, while the top line is gimped. Heart-shaped lace ends and a heart-shaped tongue complete the more feminine look.

This page, top Beautifully detailed 'Cherry' suede slip-on ankle-skimming boot with a 70mm exaggerated Louis heel and gold nappa-trimmed scallop-edged top line. The style has a wide almond toe with a heart-shaped peep toe. **bottom** High-heeled and playful, the 'Polly' court shoe appears in platinum nappa leather with a layered leather wing detail and 70mm Louis heel.

Opposite, top Original sketches for a lace-up shoe with a 70mm 1940s-inspired wide heel and wide almond toe. The ribbon-tie shoe shows Parikka's trademark heart shape, this time in the form of a cut-out on the upper. **bottom left** Design for a sling-back sandal with a 70mm heel and wide almond toe. The style features a bow-shaped strap over the toes and layers of embroidered leather to form a wing shape. **bottom right** Sketch for the 'Edith' court shoe, pictured on p. 134.

'It's all about the enjoyment of femininity.'

Minna Parikka

cable
stiching

— embroidery

sergio
rossi

Part of the Gucci Group, Sergio Rossi is not just about prestige and exclusivity, it is also based on a history of craftsmanship and the traditions of the artisan. Edmundo Castillo, senior designer for Sergio Rossi, has succeeded in encapsulating the brand's heritage by focusing on creating feminine and sexy shoes made from the finest materials.

The key to a luxurious shoe lies in its shape. High stiletto heels elongate the leg and correct the posture, while well-shaped uppers embrace a women's foot, feeling glove-like and comforting. The proportion of a shoe is so important that it can instantly transform the way a women feels – making her sexy and confident one minute or demure and intelligent the next.

All this has long fascinated Puerto Rican designer Edmundo Castillo, who spent his formative years working in upscale shoe stores in New York. 'I loved working in shoe stores because it was there that I learned how women behave when wearing a certain [type of] shoe,' Castillo says. 'I noticed that as soon as they tried them on, they started behaving differently. Their personalities seemed to change and they started walking differently. It was then that I realized how a shoe could change people and make them feel great. The beauty of a shoe is that it transforms a look and instead of just covering the feet, it takes on a whole life of its own and changes people's personalities and attitudes.' Castillo was intrigued by his observations on what women liked and desired in a shoe. '[In] high heels they walked a certain way…and with a flat "ballerina" style, they became more childish, more demure, albeit still flirty.' He decided then that he 'wanted to make beautiful shoes that women not only wanted to wear, but also to collect'.

Castillo began his formal training at Parsons School of Design in New York City and later worked with Donna Karan on both the women's and men's footwear for Donna Karan Collection. After eight years with her, Castillo joined Polo Ralph Lauren as senior director, and then returned to Donna Karan to design the Donna Karan and DKNY men's shoes. He credits the mentoring and influence of Donna Karan for much of his success. 'If it weren't for her, I wouldn't know half of what I know now,' Castillo says. He explains that she allowed him the freedom to be creative and design in his own way. 'Donna didn't just dictate what she thought I should design. She'd give me an idea and I'd take it from there. It was like being back at school,' he says.

After leaving Donna Karan in 1999, Castillo launched his own, highly successful line of shoes. In 2001, he received the Perry Ellis Award for Accessories from the highly respected Council of Fashion Designers of America and in 2004 was also nominated for American Accessory Designer of the Year. For the time being, however, Castillo has put the development of his own line on hold to concentrate on his position at Sergio Rossi.

Opposite Luxurious 100mm stiletto-heel silver sandal with hand-stitched sequins and powder-blue satin trim. The T-strap sandal fastens with several wraps of tassel-trimmed silk cord, seductively tied around the ankle.

Opposite Fuchsia suede latticework sandal with decorative gold-ring detailing, 10mm forepart platform and 100mm heel.
This page Original design sketches showing a variety of decorative evening styles.

Overleaf Burnished bronze peep-toe court shoe with 30mm forepart platform and 100mm heel. Industrial-style metallic studs accent the butterfly cut-out, while the Plexiglas heel encapsulates and reveals real gold leaf.

'Shoes change people's personalities and attitudes.'

Edmundo Castillo

Opposite and this page, top Dove-grey suede sling-back sandal with 30mm white-patent-leather-covered forepart platform and 120mm patent-covered heel. The suede upper sweeps down beneath the toes to cover the front part of the platform.
This page, bottom Glittering nude suede sandal featuring a 105mm chunky heel encrusted with a dégradé pattern of silver and gold Swarovski stones.

rupert sanderson

Worthy to be named after Narcissus himself, each of Rupert Sanderson's shoes are called a different variety of daffodil. Since launching his label in 2001, Sanderson has been dedicated to his beautifully crafted shoes, which feature elegant, hand-turned heels, exquisite skins and leathers and original colour palettes. One collection featured large Gothic bows, a technique he learned from the Queen's robe makers. 'I went there for an afternoon and learned how to make bows and rosettes, then went to Italy and taught my factory workers how to create them using heavy, stiff silks and satins.' Another collection used genuine Whitby jet, dug from the hills of Yorkshire.

Sanderson came to footwear design relatively late in life, leaving a successful job in advertising to create shoes. 'It was a cathartic thing that I just had to do,' he says. He spent several months studying and sketching before enrolling at the prestigious Cordwainers College, London. From the first day he knew that this was what he truly wanted to do and he was completely focused on why he was there. 'From the moment the doors opened in the morning to the moment they closed at night, I spent every second constantly trying to get as much making done as possible.'

Such was Sanderson's passion for learning that he spent the summer break between his first and second year on a motorbike tour of Italy, visiting all the major footwear factories along the way. Riding through the country he learned how the footwear business operates in Italy and vowed to return as soon as possible. Indeed, following his graduation, Sanderson immediately set to work with Bruno Magli in Bologna, where he 'learned the proper craft of shoemaking, by working each day in the factory making shoes'.

Despite being based in London, Rupert Sanderson is still running a Bolognese business, spending four months of each year working in Italy. Although his shoes are quintessentially English, Sanderson believes that the quality he expects in each shoe can only be achieved in Italy. He enjoys speaking daily with his chosen artisans. 'That's what excites me – the craft of making shoes. A lot of people bemoan the fact that they have to travel and spend so much time in the factory but that's what I love, dealing with people and personalities and trying to get the best product from the process. Footwear is not just a unit with a cost that needs to be in a certain place at a certain time. It is somebody's work,' he explains. This personal element is what interests Sanderson most; the relationship between himself and the people who actually make his shoes. 'They are far more interesting than being in the papers or being associated with some celebrity,' he believes. 'That world is totally against how I try to run my business as the people who make the shoes are treated terribly.' Instead, Sanderson's shoes are created for intelligent women who are confident in their own tastes and not afraid to engage with something beyond the latest celebrity-driven fad.

In the future, Sanderson hopes to continue growing his own business, including his boutique, which opened in London's Mayfair in 2004, as well as continuing his consultancy for Margaret Howell and Jean Muir footwear. 'If you are good at what you do, you are not constrained by a single style. There are sets of skills and processes, rules and restrictions but it's great to put on another jacket and work on a different line. It is, after all, about designing the best shoes you can possibly design.'

Opposite Lizard-skin 'Glitter' court shoe. See p. 155 for details.

'That's what excites me – the craft of making shoes.'

Rupert Sanderson

Page 150 Deep-red velvet 'Molly' sandal with a gold nappa trim and chunky 85mm covered heel.
Page 151, top Pink python and soft black kid tie-front Mary Jane, named 'Theo'.
This delicate style has an almond toe and a 100mm stiletto heel.
Left and page 151, bottom 'Elva' is a claret patent-leather sandal with a 105mm conical heel and a broad criss-cross strap detail.

153

Opposite and this page, bottom 'Marianne', shown here in shocking-pink satin, is Rupert Sanderson's signature evening style. The court shoe has a 100mm stiletto heel, almond toe shape and low-cut vamp with a pretty bow trim.
This page, top Olive-green 'Elvira' sandal in soft kid leather with an 85mm ship's-prow heel, criss-cross toe straps and a round toe last shape.
middle Green lizard-skin 'Glitter' court shoe with a 100mm stiletto heel, almond toe shape and low-cut vamp.

tn_29

Since she was only nine years old and designing shoes with cardboard, tape, staples and a pair of toilet-paper rolls, Tracy Neuls has been a shoe designer who demonstrates exceptional aptitude for taking the normal and mundane, and throwing them into exciting new situations. After first making a name for herself in clothing design, in both America and Europe, she eventually moved to London from Canada in 1996 to enrol at the prestigious Cordwainers College. Success came to Neuls almost instantly, and by the end of her studies she had been awarded the Royal Society of Arts award, the Absolut Cobblers award and the Blueprint/Vitra design award. Following her 1998 graduation collection, she launched her own footwear company TN_29.

The 'TN' derives from Neuls's initials, while the origin of '29' is rather more obscure: 'When I was young I was obsessed with the number 29, for no good reason,' she says. 'I doodled it everywhere I could, so when I was launching my own label I decided it was time I did something more creative with it.'

Launching her first collection in 2000, Neuls showed a unique ergonomic shape that was greeted with critical acclaim. Treating the shoe as a single form, Neuls challenged traditional footwear shapes by carrying the upper over the heel and erasing any joint. Shortly afterwards she won the New Generation Award for her innovative designs.

Neuls's priority is always to indulge feet with quality and to shatter the fashion myth that great design must be accompanied by pain. All components for her shoes are developed exclusively in Italy and she is adamant about refusing to buy ready-made or pre-designed pieces.

The beauty of Neuls's work lies not only in her use of the best craftsmen available, but also in her questioning of the expected, ignoring the rules and taking inspiration from a vast range of sources. She draws on all the fascinating everyday parts of our lives that are so often overlooked: 'It could be a sprig of green grass or a dog wagging its tail but as I walk around, it's always the simple things in life that inspire me,' she explains.

One season an entire range was based around picnics and all the shoes were packaged in boxes with tiny ants crawling out of them. Another collection was developed around broccoli. Detail is all-important and Neuls enjoys the fact that you could probably walk around in a pair of her shoes for months before realizing that there is a little imprint of a map to her shop on the sole.

Opening her first boutique in 2005 in London's Marylebone, Neuls says the experience has been a revelation. 'It's amazing that you can have such a good rapport with someone you don't even know. Everyone who comes through the door is lovely. They are people who are truly interested in design.'

It is no surprise that Neuls's boutique attracts a clientele who are passionate about design, as she has applied the same radical philosophy to her shop display as to her footwear designs. Inside, shoes are freed from the constraints of shelving and hang everywhere. According to Neuls, 'My shoes are whole objects, not half stories and that's how they should be experienced. I want people to be able to explore and play with them, and see them in the 360-degree context they were meant for.'

Opposite 'Peep toe Polly' style in jute. See p. 159 for details.

Opposite and this page, middle left
'Robin', with its 60mm heel, is a 360-degree shoe experience, from the heel and the twisted toe shape to the lining and the sole. The insole is printed to resemble worn gold vintage shoes and each shoe is signed by its primary craftsman on the sole.

This page, top left Open-toe 'Peep toe Polly' style in jute with a 50mm red nappa-covered hooked heel, double buckle detailing and red trim. With a nod to orthopaedic shoes, an interesting juxtaposition is made between the clinical and the sexy line of the shoe.
bottom left Vintage-inspired, this court shoe with its 60mm heel and twisted toe shape forms part of a limited-edition series using late-1940s cotton prints and gold nappa linings.
right column Original design sketches.

Overleaf Red pigskin 'Button Betty' court shoe with a 60mm hooked heel and rounded toe shape. Inspired by an octopus toy the designer played with as a child, this shoe is technically very challenging to make. The button forms part of the leather as it is wrapped into the upper and twisted within, rather than being sewn on top.

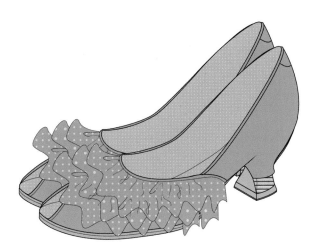

159

'My shoes are whole objects, not half stories.'

Tracy Neuls

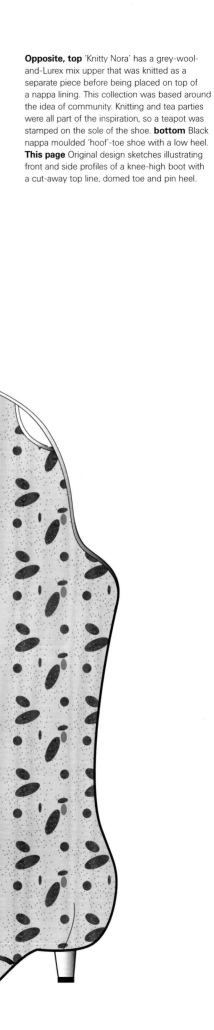

Opposite, top 'Knitty Nora' has a grey-wool-and-Lurex mix upper that was knitted as a separate piece before being placed on top of a nappa lining. This collection was based around the idea of community. Knitting and tea parties were all part of the inspiration, so a teapot was stamped on the sole of the shoe. **bottom** Black nappa moulded 'hoof'-toe shoe with a low heel. **This page** Original design sketches illustrating front and side profiles of a knee-high boot with a cut-away top line, domed toe and pin heel.

marloes
ten bhömer

Marloes ten Bhömer's groundbreaking designs are derived from her fascination with the intricacies of modern machinery. By exploring the space between their exterior and internal workings, Bhömer illustrates how designers can escape from the traditional conventions of form. 'Mystery is my inspiration,' she says. She describes the 'inherent logic and mystery in machines and their highly specific language of efficiency. This language has as much to do with concealing as it has with revealing, and within this contradiction lies a multitude of opportunities for interpretation.' Bhömer's work investigates this void.

Her nonconformist attitude was first developed at the Arnhem School of Arts in her native Holland and later at the Royal College of Art in London, where she chose to pursue product design over footwear design. As a product designer Bhömer finds shoes a very interesting and complex subject matter. 'Footwear design combines a full spectrum of design concerns, from material knowledge to engineering,' she says. In addition, her highly intuitive approach deals with designing objects that ignore or criticize convention in order to make the product world less generic.

Undoubtedly left of mainstream, Bhömer's work continually pushes the boundaries of conventional design in pursuit of undiscovered territory. Bhömer's experimental ventures into the unknown boast remarkable variety in design and materials and are unconstrained by the practicalities of footwear. Carbon fibre, stainless steel, Tyvek and fibreglass are assembled with construction techniques borrowed from other design fields. These include rapid prototyping, metal pressing, wet moulding and a 'leather-mâché' technique, which she invented to enable her to create shoes whose interior traces the form of the foot whilst 'redefining the exterior'.

Inspired by designs that show consideration and logic, Bhömer is particularly influenced by the Cheetah, a prosthetic leg manufactured by Flex Foot Inc. She describes it as 'a great piece of work because the designers didn't just try to emulate legs or normal prosthetics. Instead they thought about how they could improve on the human leg rather than making the same shape that we always use.'

Similarly, Bhömer hopes to redefine how consumers perceive footwear by creating fully functional footwear that defies the conventions of everyday shoes. 'Life is so boring; we understand how products work, we have seen them all before. What really fascinates me is when you understand what the product is but at the same time it doesn't look like anything you have ever seen before,' she says.

At present, Bhömer has only produced one-off designs, which are pieces of art and designed to be exhibited in galleries. Her greatest challenge will come when creating experimental yet technically sound shoes, something she is currently pursuing with UK-based footwear brand United Nude (see p. 178). Bhömer is looking forward to the future. 'I am very excited about the footwear industry,' she says, 'as there are more and more designers experimenting with production techniques.' Like Bhömer, such designers are challenging what shoes can be.

Opposite Leather-mâché shoe. See p. 166 for details.

This page, top Elephant-blue leather-mâché shoe with an 80mm stainless-steel stiletto heel. Leather mâché, a laminating technique invented and developed by Marloes ten Bhömer, has been used to construct this style. The technique uses butter-soft nappa leather and makes it possible to vary the thickness of the shoe; although the inside traces the shape of the foot exactly, the outside form can be more abstract. **bottom** Red shoe created using Ten Bhömer's leather-mâché technique. In this shoe extra large sheets of leather are used, making the form even more abstract.

Opposite, top Sketches for rubber SLS (Selective Laser Sintering) rapid-prototyped shoe from a three-dimensional computer drawing. This style is completely designed and constructed using a computer-aided prototyping/manufacturing technique. **bottom** Sand-coloured and square-toed, this shoe has an 85mm heel and is made from carbon fibre and kid leather. The carbon fibre is leather-laminated in a three-piece mould and the heel is incorporated into the flat side panel of the shoe.

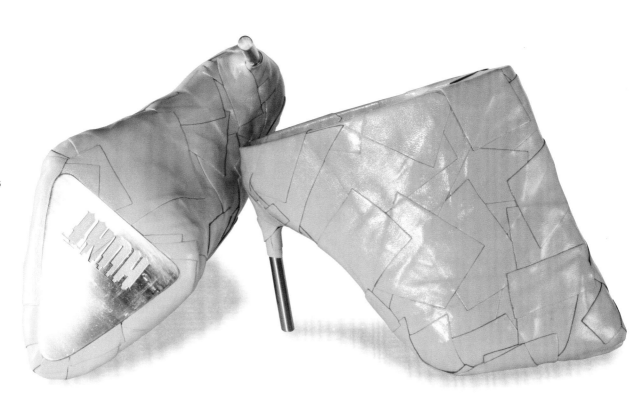

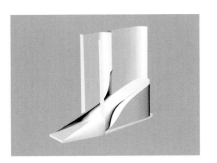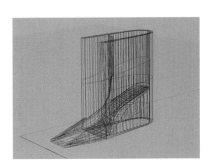

This page Cut and folded white tarpaulin shoe with a 99mm solid birch-wood heel and square toe. The upper has been made from one piece of tarpaulin, which, rather than being stretched over the last to mould the shoe, has been left to fold loosely.

Opposite Heel-less shoe in ivory polyurethane resin that has been cast in a two-piece mould. The shoe traces the form of the foot exactly on the interior, while the exterior shape is more abstract. This style can also be walked in on tiptoe.

'Mystery is my inspiration.'

Marloes ten Bhömer

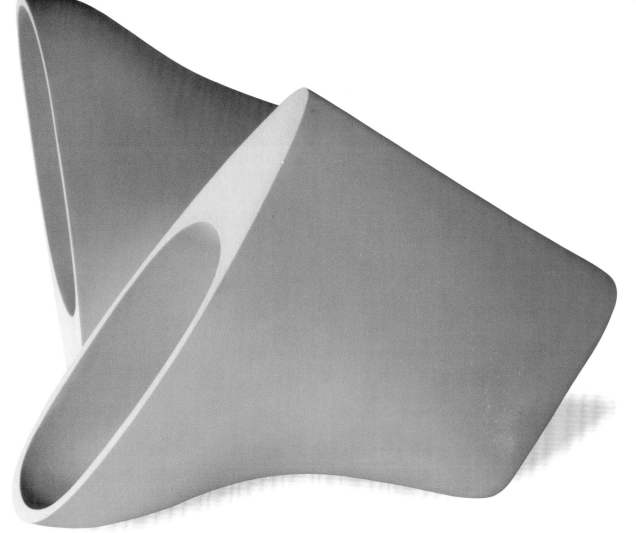

terra plana

Unfazed by the challenges ahead, Terra Plana aims to create the world's most innovative and ecologically friendly footwear brand by 2010. By fusing traditional shoemaking with ecologically sound materials, they have struck a perfect balance, successfully creating highly directional footwear with a conscience.

Initially Dutch, the brand was founded by Charles Berman in 1989, then sold to Lance Clark (sixth generation of Clarks shoes) in 1998, before relaunching in 2001 with his son Galahad JD Clark (see p. 179) at the helm. Galahad was joined in 2004 by creative director Ajoy Sahu (formerly of Premiata and Prada) and by designer Asher Clark (2004 Young Shoe Designer of the Year) in 2005.

Terra Plana's ecological approach is all-encompassing, addressing everything from manufacture and material use to packaging and exporting. Coffee bags, jackets, shirts, jeans and leftover leather scraps from the car industry are all happily recycled into shoes. In addition, almost all of Terra Plana's leathers are treated with a chrome-free tanning system and the wood used for the heels of the shoes is sourced from protected and sustainably run forests. They also use recycled card for their shoe boxes and aim to ship everything by boat, thus minimizing air freight. Furthermore, by using stitched constructions, such as welting, sachetto, true mocassin, turned shoe, blake and side stitch, Terra Plana minimizes the need for glue, which reduces toxins. All shoes are handmade in studios employing Fair Trade principles, where employees are taught a trade rather than simply working on a production line.

With seven generations of shoemakers behind him, Galahad Clark has become a major authority on 'green'

design, combining experience and knowledge with a keen eye for changing customer culture. As he says, 'Sustainability makes perfect business sense and will continue to be a defining characteristic of successful businesses in the future.' Business models are one thing, but it is Terra Plana's acute understanding of modern lifestyles that is the driving force. Creative director Sahu explains, 'The demand is for new and exciting products, which we are addressing and subsequently succeeding in providing.'

For designer Asher Clark, his current interest lies in designing footwear that is eco-friendly yet directional: 'I'm not talking hemp sandals for eco warriors; I'm talking beautiful products in eco-alternative materials.' Sahu adds, 'Rather than obeying trends all the time, I think we must become a brand that has a lot of style and a lot of grace. What we do is done with passion and is generally timeless.'

Terra Plana ably demonstrates, to those who suggest that sustainability is neither economically based nor economically feasible, that success can be compatible with caring for the environment and, perhaps even more surprisingly, that it is possible without compromising design.

Opposite Silk-printed 'Orchid' ankle-wrap sandal with crossed-lattice detailing on the leather-covered heel.

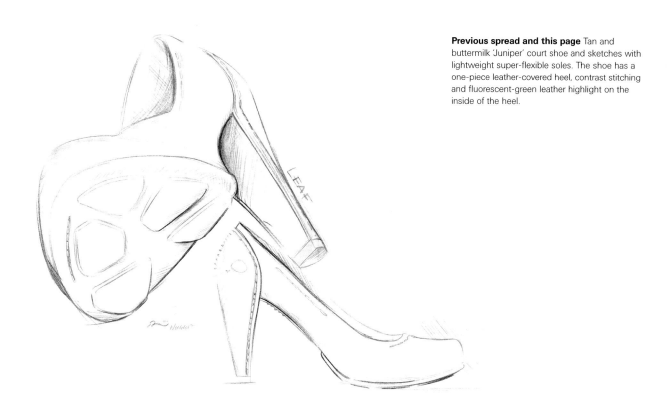

Previous spread and this page Tan and buttermilk 'Juniper' court shoe and sketches with lightweight super-flexible soles. The shoe has a one-piece leather-covered heel, contrast stitching and fluorescent-green leather highlight on the inside of the heel.

Bitter-chocolate and white fleece-lined 'Maple' ankle boot, again with a one-piece leather-covered heel and fluorescent-green contrast stitching and leather highlight on the inside of the heel.

This page, top Environmentally aware, the Ghillie court shoe has a sustainable-wood stacked heel and a nubuck and recycled coffee-bean-bag upper. The style also has a whip-stitched toe and heel upper. **bottom** Pull-on 'Janis' western-style boot with a sustainable-wood heel. The upper is made of nubuck and recycled coffee bean bags with a leather heel counter, contrast stitching and pull-on tabs.

Opposite Vegetable-tanned 'Viana' boot constructed from locally sourced materials to minimize the need for transportation. The boot has a blake-stitched construction giving it a smart, clean look.

'What we do is done with passion and is generally timeless.' Ajoy Sahu

united nude

Disillusioned by the impersonal nature of large-scale, monolithic buildings, Dutch architect Rem D Koolhaas came to footwear design after looking to break away and pursue his work in smaller, more intimate proportions. Koolhaas, not to be confused with his uncle, renowned architect Rem Koolhaas, collaborated with pioneering shoemaker Galahad JD Clark (seventh generation of Clarks shoes, see p. 170) to create United Nude. The pair specialize in creating conceptual footwear interpretations of architecture and the fluid lines of quintessential design objects. The name United Nude reflects the philosophy of the brand. 'involvement in projects with international teams (united) in an open way with direct recognition (nude)'.

Upon launching their brand, the pair first introduced the revolutionary 'Mobius' shoe, inspired both by the eponymous mathematical form, the Mobius strip, and by a desire to reinterpret Mies van der Rohe's 'Barcelona' chair as footwear. This shoe, with no beginning or end, comprises one continuous piece, simultaneously functioning as the footbed, upper and heel. Other styles include the Eamz, which pays homage to the creative couple Charles and Ray Eames; the cast-aluminium foot that is found on a number of their furniture classics is reinterpreted here as the heel. And, the Porn design has a functioning footbed suspended through a loop, which acts as both the heel and upper.

Koolhaas still regards himself as an architect, despite co-running a company that only designs shoes. 'I see the shoes as a form of architecture; as it is one of the largest-scale levels of design it's therefore much easier to scale down than to scale up.' Koolhaas freely admits to being influenced by modernism, an aesthetic the designer strives to reflect with United Nude. In true modernist style, his goal is to break the seasonal cycle by channelling effort into creating timeless classics, which are fresh, comfortable and affordable to an eager public excited about well-designed functional products.

While Koolhaas and Clark largely choose to ignore trends they do update existing styles with new materials and heel heights seasonally. That said, United Nude is still about as far removed from traditional shoemaking as it is possible to be. With conventional footwear factories unable to cope with the technical specifications of their designs, the pair were forced to look further afield. Their search led them to the production lines of the aviation and automotive industries, ironically also forcing these industries to consider smaller and more intimate design.

Having firmly established their footwear foundations, the creative duo are eager to pursue other avenues of design, with the possible development of clothing, eyewear, bags and furniture to add to their revolutionary brand.

Opposite Black micro-fibre 'Sharp' padded bubble boot with drawstring top line.

Sketch and views of the 'Mobius' shoe in
pink polished calf. The shoe, inspired by
the Mobius strip, was United Nude's original
launch product. It features a single band,
which is at once the sole, heel, footbed and
upper of the shoe.

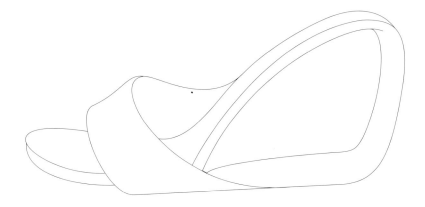

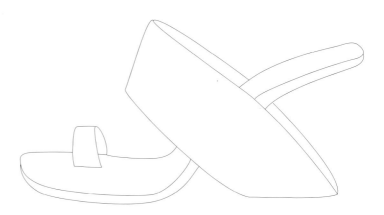

Overleaf and this page, top and middle
Sketch and views of the 'Porn' shoe in black
leather with a toe loop. This style is fashioned
from a simple concept, which sees the footbed
floating through a loop that functions as both
the heel and upper.
This page, bottom The 'Porn' shoe with a
triple strap.

This page and opposite, bottom
Sketch and views of the 'Eamz' shoe, which is conceptually linked to the classic furniture designs of Charles and Ray Eames. The black moulded-rubber shoe incorporates the signature Eames' chair foot used as the heel and made from steel.
Opposite, top A thong variation of the 'Eamz' shoe.

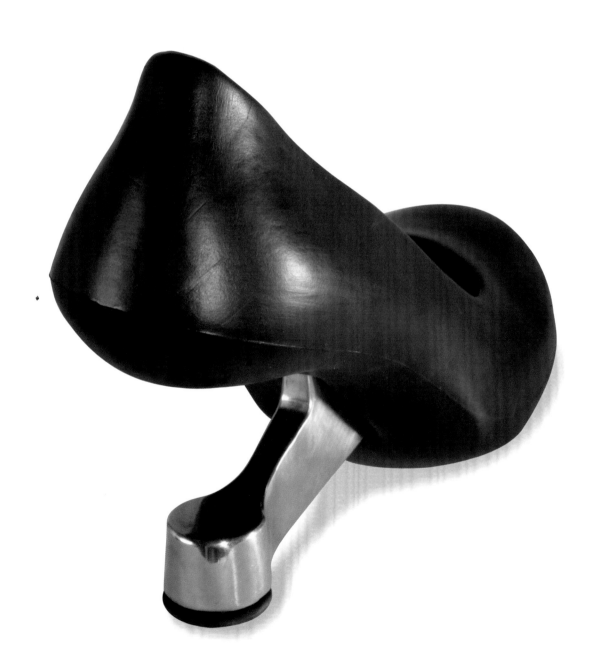

'I see shoes as a form of architecture.'

Rem D Koolhaas

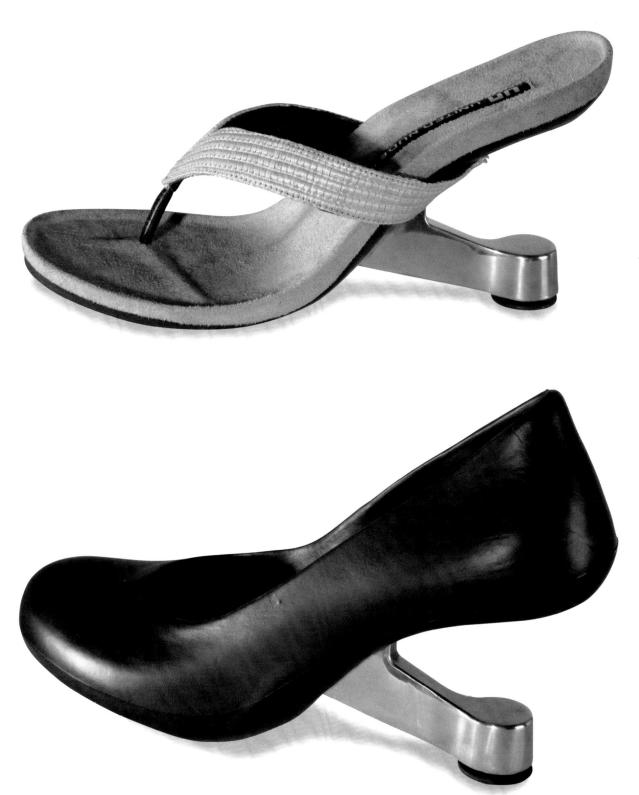

michel vivien

When Michel Vivien began designing for renowned designer Michel Perry in 1990, Perry said to him, 'I want you to design beautiful shoes for beautiful women'. Vivien has never forgotten this statement and has continued to develop luxurious footwear that fits this brief perfectly.

Naturally, the heel is all-important to Vivien's silhouette, although he refuses prudently to create them agonizingly high: 'Possibly ten centimetres for evening wear, and in exceptional cases eleven to impress the journalists, but never any higher.' This pragmatic approach is refreshing, as Vivien, describing his style as 'Parisian, sober and balanced', believes that shoes must not only be beautiful, but also wearable and comfortable.

His signature designs feature the softest nappa leather and fine-quality calfskin in tender colours such as honey, powder pink, chestnut and bone. Strips of woven leather 'cage' the foot, creating a striking silhouette that is sexy and seductive without appearing too aggressive. 'Luxury is not just about big brands,' he says. 'You have to be able to touch it, feel it and smell it.'

Vivien works with the finest artisan craftsmen available, asserting that 'there is no point in creating a shoe if you are not going to execute it beautifully'. At the start of his career, he bore witness to the unfortunate decline of the French luxury footwear industry, which has now almost disappeared. Today he is equally concerned about the difficulties that are facing the few remaining Italian craftsmen, saying, 'I would like to continue to provide comfort and luxury for the women who wear my shoes, but it will only be possible if the traditions of the artisan survive.'

After attending the Pierre Alechinsky Fine Art courses at the Ecole des Beaux Arts in Paris, Vivier worked for such prestigious designers as Carel, Michel Perry, Charles Jourdan and Sergio Rossi (see p. 140). He also designed for the houses of Christian Dior, Thierry Mugler (for whom he created his renowned ultra-sexy latex thigh-high boots with studded heels), Givenchy, Christian Lacroix and Yves Saint Laurent Haute Couture. He began designing under his own name in 1998, and worked as the artistic director for Robert Clergerie from 2003 to 2005.

In 2006 Vivien took an important new step in his career. Not content with opening his first boutique in the 1st arrondissement of Paris, just a step away from the heart of the Palais Royal, he also began a successful collaboration with Alber Elbaz, designing the shoe collection for the house of Lanvin. 'I have got so much satisfaction from my collaboration with Elbaz,' he says, 'that I would like it to continue alongside the development of my own label.'

Opposite Black python court shoe. See p. 188 for details.

This page Original design sketches for a range of shoe styles.

Opposite, top left Black python almond-toe court shoe with python-covered heel. **bottom left** Rear view of a high sculpted-heel court shoe with an almond toe shape, split heel upper and ankle-strap fastening. **right** Beautifully simple and classic tan pull-on leather knee-high boot. The boot has a worn patina, block heel and almond toe shape.

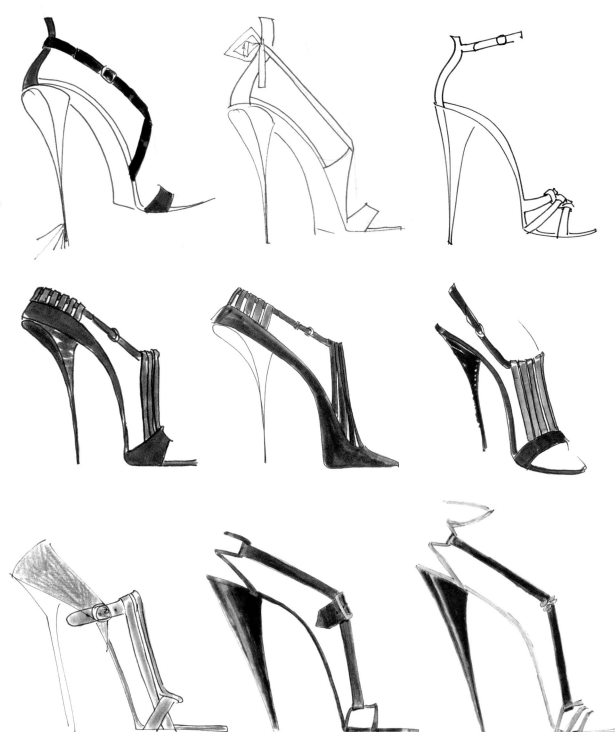

'You have to be able to touch luxury, feel it and smell it.'

Michel Vivien

Previous spread and this page, bottom
Gold goatskin sandal with a latticework T-strap
and ankle tie.
Opposite and this page, top Golden-yellow
satin and black leather sandal with a caged heel
and ankle-strap fastening.

walk that walk

French footwear designers Nicolas Berney and Alain Demore believe that fashion should not only be fun but also a little bit challenging. It is only right, therefore, that they design their quirky collections accordingly and, as a result, have developed a reputation for creating footwear that combines wit with commercial wisdom.

The duo launched their brand Walk that Walk in 2003, with a nautical but nice summer collection presented during Paris Fashion Week. This first collection was more conceptual than commercial, exploring the possibilities of the modern beach sandal. Materials ranged from luxurious shark hide to neoprene and the rubberized canvas more commonly found on inflatable mattresses. Heel and sole shapes were directly inspired from surfboard fins and the lacquered hulls of sailing boats, while colours were reminiscent of sun-drenched skin. If the collection had had a smell to it, Demore says, 'it would have been, without a doubt, the sweet scent of holidays and Hawaiian Tropic tanning oil!'

This first collection received a very positive reaction from the press and industry insiders, and Walk that Walk have outdone themselves with each subsequent collection. Themes have included everything from the French bourgeoisie and the passion of La Dolce Vita to carefree childhood summers and boudoir chic. Walk that Walk have also reinterpreted the Kickers classic lace-up ankle boots and Aigle's timeless rubber Wellingtons.

Berney and Demore ensure that each collection achieves the perfect balance between style and commercial necessity by manufacturing their shoes in Italy using luxurious and often quirky materials. They are particularly conscious of the current changes facing the footwear industry in that country. 'Mass market items are being produced in the Far East or in countries where labour costs are low, but the quality, reactivity and culture of high-end craftsmanship in Italy still suits our need for perfectly made luxury fashion shoes.' They admit, however, that they have to remain open to new opportunities, saying that 'if Italy reached the standards of quality that were once only available in France or Britain, why couldn't China reach them one day too?'

Both designers absconded to footwear design from previous careers – Berney from advertising design and Demore from design and marketing – and both have used their previous experiences to aid their ascent. Having attended the Fashion Institute of Technology in New York, they 'acquired basic skills', then moved back to Paris to concentrate on their 'serious' training.

The pair have long been fans of Alber Elbaz, describing his work as 'perfection'. They also admire shoe designer Tokio Kumagai 'for his wittiness' and legendary designer Roger Vivier, whose work Berney says 'has made it difficult for all designers to come up with anything better'. The designers also take inspiration from sportswear and credit Nike for creating 'some of the most beautiful sneakers in the world during the mid-1990s'.

Berney and Demore aim to build on the Walk that Walk brand in the future by launching a menswear line and opening their first boutique.

Opposite Zesty orange tumble-grain leather sandal with an asymmetric vamp, decorative leather-covered buckle and 80mm wooden stiletto heel.

'Craftsmanship in Italy suits our need for perfectly made luxury fashion shoes.'

Nicolas Berney and Alain Demore

Page 196 and this page Rose-red sandal with an 80mm pink patent-leather-covered heel, interlocking leather chain-like linked upper and multi-wrap ankle strap.
Page 197, top left Sketch for a forepart platform sandal with decorative rose detail and a chunky 80mm heel. **top right** Original design for a T-strap sandal with an 80mm stiletto heel and multi-button appliqué decoration on the upper. **bottom left** Design for an open-toe sandal with forepart platform sole and a fully covered 80mm heel. Joins are erased between heel and upper, while petal-shaped cut-outs on the upper reveal toe cleavage. **bottom right** Sketch for an open-toe sandal with decorative latticework ankle-strap detail and an 80mm stiletto heel.

This page and overleaf Citron suede 80mm stiletto sandal with mirrored metallic heel upper and bold industrial-style cut-outs.

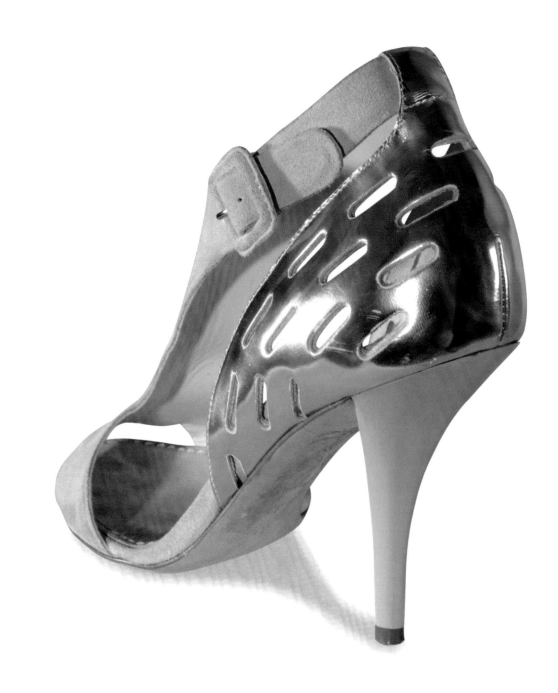

Glossary

A

Ankle wrap Straps that are worn wrapped and tied around the ankle.

Apron toe A type of toe characterized by a large overlay that covers the front of the toe and has visible edges or stitching and that forms an apron on the front of the shoe.

B

Backstay Reinforcement of the vertical seam at the back of a shoe with a narrow piece of leather.

Ball heel A spherical heel.

Ballerina shoe Soft, low kid shoe with thin sole and flat heel, sometimes made with drawstring throat. Inspired by the shoes worn by ballet dancers.

Ballet laces Wide satin ribbons used as lacings for ballet slippers, criss-crossing at intervals around the ankle and calf and tied in a bow.

Bicycle toe Type of toe characterized by two stitched straight-line accents, so named because of their similarity to professional bicycling shoe detailing.

Blake stitch Part of the shoe manufacturing process invented by Lyman Blake in 1861, in which the upper is pulled around the last and fastened to the insole by means of tacks. The outsole is then attached by stitching or by cementing. It is a very secure construction, which has a smart, clean look. Also called McKay shoe construction.

Blucher toe A type of toe characterized by a smooth, turned stitch border around the toe area, like an apron toe style in reverse.

Boat shoe A type of shoe originally meant to be worn aboard a boat, usually with a siped, non-slip outsole, often with side lacing details.

Boulevard heel Sturdy high heel similar to a Cuban heel that is tapered at the sides and back; has a straight front and a flange where the heel joins with the sole.

Brogue A heavy walking shoe, originally made for men, that usually has a wing tip decorated with heavy perforations and pinking.

C

Cap toe A type of toe style with a full toe overlay and a straight stitching line across the top part of the toe, often seen in dress shoes.

Chelsea boot A type of boot, usually ankle height, in a pull-on style with elastic side panels.

Chrome tanning A method of tanning leather using sodium dichromate.

Chunky heel A high or medium heel that has an exaggerated width.

Cigarette heel Tall, slender heel shaped like a cigarette.

Cleats Any traction-enhancing spikes or nubs attached to the sole of an athletic shoe, often used in grass-based sports to ensure steady footing.

Clog A type of shoe, usually casual and comfortable, with an open or closed heel and a slip-on style.

Columnar heel High circular-style heel that is round and column-shaped.

Comma heel Heel that curves inwards like a reverse comma.

Continental heel High, narrow heel made straight in front with square corners at base and slight curve at back.

Counter A piece of heavy leather or other stiffening material inserted between the outside and the lining of the upper at the back part of the shoe. The purpose of the counter is to strengthen the back part of the shoe and to prevent it from sagging and losing its shape.

Court shoe British term for pump.

Covered heel Heel of wood or plastic covered with leather or another plastic.

Crêpe sole A type of rubber sole characterized by a nubbly texture like crêpe paper.

Crescent toe A narrow-toed shoe ending with a curved rather than a needle toe.

Croc embossed Leather that has been embossed or stamped in a pattern simulating crocodile skin.

Cuban heel A medium to high broad heel with a slight curve at the back.

Cube heel A square-backed heel.

Cut-outs Shapes cut out of the upper to create an open-air effect.

D

Dégradé The French term for 'faded'.

Devoré A technique that leaves a raised pattern on fabric by using chemicals to dissolve part of the fabric's pile while leaving other pile areas and the ground intact. Often used on velvet.

Distressed leather Leather that has been rubbed, scratched or treated for a worn effect.

E

Espadrille Any shoe that has woven rope or rope-look trim, usually in the sole area.

203

F

Faux leather Simulated, non-animal, leather-like material, usually polyurethane.

Fisherman sandal Type of sandal with woven or stitched vertical and horizontal straps, often with a closed toe.

Flat heel Shoes with a very low or no heel height.

Flip-flop A type of sandal, usually a thong, with a lightweight foam outsole that makes a flip-flop sound when you walk.

Footbed The insole of the shoe, where the foot rests.

Forepart Part of the shoe or last from the shank forward and including the ball and toe.

Foxing Leather sewn on at the top of the back seam for reinforcement and decoration.

Full-grain leather Leather that shows a natural texture or grain.

G

Ghillie Laced shoe, usually without a tongue, with rounded laces pulling through leather loops and fastened around the ankle.

Gimping The zig-zag crocodile-teeth style of cutting on the edge of some shoes is called gimping. It is machine cut, much like on a sewing machine, and serves not only as a decoration, but also to make weakly cut edges more palatable. Also called pinking or saw-toothed.

H

Haircalf Natural calfskin material with a soft furry texture.

Hardware Any solid metal or plastic fittings, which are used on the shoe as a fastening or for decoration, for example, buckles, chains and studs.

Harness boot A type of boot characterized by straps across the instep and heel, usually joined by a ring detail.

Heel cup A piece of leather (part of the upper) on the outside of the back of the shoe covering the seam joining the quarters. It may be a narrow strip or a long vertical piece of leather in line with the heel.

I

Inlay Leather or fabric placed below a cut-out layer and stitched into place for decorative effect.

Insole The part of the shoe that the foot rests upon, usually cushioned.

Instep The area of the foot between the toes and the ankle, or the top front part of a shoe.

K

Kitten heel A type of heel that is set forward, usually at a low height.

L

Last A block or form shaped like a human foot and used when making or repairing shoes.

Last shapes A variety of shapes used to accommodate different foot types. They are related to the height of the arch, for example, a curved last is used for high-arched feet and a straight last is used for low-arched feet. Other categories include semi-straight, slightly curved and semi-curved, although there is no defined parameter for the distinction between shapes.

Lasting The shaping or moulding of the upper tightly to the contours of the last.

Leather The dressed or tanned hide of an animal, usually with the hair removed.

Lining The material inside a shoe.

Lug sole A sole with a heavy three-dimensional traction pattern.

Louis heel Heel of medium height curved sharply inwards around sides and back, then flared slightly at base, similar to heels worn in Louis xv period in France.

M

Mary Jane A type of women's shoe characterized by a strap across the instep.

Midsole The part of the shoe between the very bottom and where the foot rests, often cushioned.

Moccasin Heel-less shoe in which the sole is made of leather and comes up to form the quarter and part of the vamp. A tongue-like curved piece is hand stitched to complete the vamp.

Monk strap A type of shoe designed like an Oxford, but with a strap closure across the instep rather than a lace-up front closure.

Motorcycle boot Boots ideal for riding a motorcycle, often with thick, durable soles.

Mudguard Separate application of leather to the upper just above the sole and sometimes extending all around the foot. First designed to protect the upper from dampness.

Mule A closed-toe shoe with no back.

N

Nappa leather A type of leather characterized by its stretchy, soft, smooth texture.

Needle toe Long, narrow, extremely pointed toe.

Negative heel Popular in comfort footwear, a type of footbed with a lowered heel area designed for more natural foot placement.

Nubuck A type of leather that has been bucked or sanded for a smooth texture with a slight nap.

O

Open-toed shoe Women's shoe with the toe section cut out.

Outsole Bottom part of a shoe that touches the ground.

Overlay Detailing on a shoe made by layering material on top of other material.

Oxford A low shoe that is laced over the instep.

P

Patent leather A type of leather that has been varnished for a shiny finish.

Peekaboo toe A type of closed toe with a small open panel allowing a glimpse of toe.

Pinking Detailing characterized by a sawtooth edge.

Platform sole Midsole of shoe, which raises the foot off the ground on a platform of varying heights.

Plissé A crinkled, pebbly surface created by shrinking fabric in small areas, while untreated parts remain the same size.

Pumps Women's dress shoes, usually slip-on, often with enclosed toe and sides.

Pyramid heel Medium-high heel with squared base flaring towards the sole like an inverted pyramid.

Q

Quarter The part of a shoe upper above the vamp line. It may also be split into several component parts, such as foxing and heel cup.

Quarter lining The upper lining at the back part of the shoe extending forward to the vamp line.

Quarter panel The sides of the shoe from the heel to the toe.

R

Rand A leather strip placed between the shoe upper and the sole.

Ruched A type of detailing characterized by gathered or pleated material with stitching accents.

S

Sachetto This shoe has a lining that is stitched like a moccasin and then the upper is lasted over the lining and Blake stitched through. The look is smart but has the feel of a moccasin.

Saddle seam Hand- or machine-stitched seam used on shoes when two raw edges of leather stand up on the outside.

Sandal Originally a shoe attached to the foot by thongs. Today any open shoe where the upper consists of any decorative or functional arrangement of straps. A sandal can be foot-low to knee-high, with any heel height, and is designed for simple utility or casual wear, or as a fashion shoe.

Scalloped A type of detailing characterized by round, wavy edges.

Sculpted heel A type of high heel moulded in one piece, usually out of high-impact plastic.

Shank The part of the sole between the heel and the ball. It is usually reinforced with material of sufficient rigidity to support the weight of the wearer.

Ship's-prow heel A narrow heel shaped like a ship's prow.

Shoe Outer covering for the foot that does not reach higher than the ankle. Shoes are basically made up of the sole, the vamp, the quarter and the shank.

Side stitch Units are stitched to the side of the shoe, creating a 'mudguard effect' so that the upper sits in a very safe 'cup'.

Siped A type of outsole with narrow grooves to prevent slipping.

Sling back Shoes that are backless with a rear strap that goes around the upper heel, usually with a buckle or elastic panel.

Slouched Shoes with a baggy, gathered design that slouches down, usually found in boots.

Sole Another word for outsole, the bottom part of the shoe.

Stacked heel A heel that has horizontal lines, indicating that it is made up of stacked layers of leather, or a heel with that appearance.

Stiletto A high, tapered, narrow heel, also called a spike heel, named after the knife of the same name.

Stingray Exotic leather from the skin of a stingray.

Strappy sandal A sandal characterized by a multiple strap design.

Suede Leather that has been sanded or roughed to produce a surface with a soft texture.

Sueded fabric Fabric that has been given a soft nap to simulate the feel of suede leather.

T

Thong sandal Any sandal that has material that fits between the toes, especially the big and second toes.

Toe box The roofed area over and around the part of the shoe that covers the toes.

Toe ridge A horizontal ridge added to the footbed of some sandals to anchor and provide support and cushioning for the toes.

Toe-thong post The part of a thong sandal that actually fits between the toes.

Tongue The flap of material under the laces or buckles of a shoe.

Top line The edge of the upper around the throat of the shoe or boot usually finished by binding or other means.

T-strap A type of shoe with a single vertical strap linking the toe and ankle/heel areas.

Turned shoe A shoe made inside out with a basic sole between the foot and the ground. The upper and soles of turned shoes are very flexible. The turned shoe last is designed in a single size and then a set is made in the range of sizes and widths in which shoes are to be manufactured.

U

Upper The part of the shoe that covers the top part of the foot, from heel to toe.

V

Vachetta leather A type of soft cow leather.

Vamp The front centre part of a shoe's upper.

Vegetable-tanned leather A natural alternative to chrome tanning. The leather is prepared using vegetable extracts that create beautiful deep colours.

W

Waist The section around the feet, last or shoe between the ball and instep.

Wedge heel Slanted heel made in one piece with the sole of the shoe. Comes in low, medium and high heights.

Wellington boot Calf length or below the knee boot with a seam below the ankle making it look like a top has been joined to a man's low shoe. Usually waterproof. Named after the Duke of Wellington who defeated Napoleon in the battle of Waterloo in 1815.

Welt A narrow strip of leather stitched to a shoe between the upper and the sole. The 'Goodyear' welt is a construction in which the joining of the upper and sole is done so as to form a very firm attachment and a perfectly smooth insole.

Welted shoe Any shoe using a welt, or strip of material, to join the upper to the sole.

Wing cap Heart-shaped toecap.

Contact details

Nicole Brundage
Showroom/Press Office Address:
And Studio
Via Pietro Colletta 69
20137 Milan, Italy
Telephone: +39 02 45487375
Email: andreapilastro@andstudio.it
www.nicolebrundage.com

Marco Censi
Via G. Uberti 24
20129 Milan, Italy
Telephone: +39 02 45495761
Email: contact@marcocensi.com
www.marcocensi.com

Adele Clarke
Telephone: +44 796 620 9789

Diego Dolcini
DO.IT SRL
Via Goito 16
40132 Bologna, Italy
Telephone: +39 051 270442
Email: info@diegodolcini.it
www.diegodolcini.it

Finsk
Telephone: +44 793 913 7643
Email: info@finsk.com
www.julia@finsk.com

Bruno Frisoni
20 Boulevard Poissonnière
75009 Paris, France
Telephone: +33 142 65 20 40
Email: office@brunofrisoni.com
www.brunofrisoni.com

Pierre Hardy
Store:
156 Galerie De Valois
Jardins Du Palais Royal
75001 Paris, France
Telephone: +33 142 60 59 75
Office:
63 Rue De Lancry
75010 Paris, France
Telephone: +33 153 19 11 19
www.pierrehardy.com

Guillaume Hinfray
Via G. Uberti 24
20129 Milan, Italy
Telephone: +39 02 45495761
Email: contact@guillaumehinfray.com
www.guillaumehinfray.com

Jenne O
322a Hackney Road
London E2 7AX, UK
Telephone: +44 207 729 9937
Email: info@jenneo.com
www.jenneo.com

Max Kibardin
Via Bezzecca 1
20135 Milan, Italy
Telephone: +39 02 36555547
Email: kibardin@fastwebnet.it

Nicholas Kirkwood
Telephone: +44 208 788 2106
Email: sales.pr@nicholaskirkwood.com
www.nicholaskirkwood.com

Laetitia'S
La Palma, 43 2° Ext. Izda
28004 Madrid, Spain
Email: info@laetitias.com
www.laetitias.com

LD Tuttle
12733 Parkyns St
Los Angeles, CA 90049, USA
Telephone: +1 917 301 0674
Email: info@ldtuttle.com
www.ldtuttle.com

Benoît Méléard
18 Avenue Gabriel Péri
93400 Saint-Ouen, France
Telephone: +33 149 23 79 79
(Agent: Kuki de Salvertes at Totem)
Email: benoit@totemfashion.com
www.totemfashion.com

Chie Mihara
AVD Camilo Jose Cela
42 Bajos Elda
03600 Alicante, Spain
Telephone: +34 96 698 0415
Email: comercial@chiemihara.com
www.chiemihara.com

MIHARAYASUHIRO
2-3-7 Sendagaya Shibuya-Ku
Tokyo 151-0051, Japan
Telephone: +81 3 5775 7143
Email: noe2000@sosu.co.jp
www.sosu.co.jp

Minna Parikka
Email: press@minnaparikka.com
www.minnaparikka.com

Sergio Rossi
Sergio Rossi spa
Via Montenapoleone 9
20121 Milan, Italy
Telephone: +39 02 7632081
Email: Xavier.rougeaux@sergiorossi.it
www.sergiorossi.it

Rupert Sanderson
33 Bruton Place, Mayfair
London W1J 6NP, UK
Telephone: +44 870 750 9181
www.rupertsanderson.co.uk

TN_29
29 Marylebone Lane
London W1 2NQ, UK
Telephone: +44 207 935 0039
Email: info@tn29.com
www.tn29.com

Marloes ten Bhömer
Marloes ten Bhömer Studios
Unit 1, 16 Telford Road
London W10 5SH, UK
Telephone: +44 778 650 5661
Email: marloes@marloestenbhomer.com
www.marloestenbhomer.com

Terra Plana and United Nude
Head office:
124 Bermondsey Street
London SE1 3TX, UK
Concept store:
64 Neal Street, Covent Garden
London, WC2H 9PQ, UK
Telephone: +44 207 407 3758
Email: melissa@terraplana.com
cedric@unitednude.com
www.terraplana.com
www.unitednude.com

Michel Vivien
Store:
15 rue Molière
75001 Paris, France
Telephone: +33 142 96 38 20
Office:
6 rue de Nice
75011 Paris, France
Telephone: +33 143 70 50 88
Email: michelvivien@msn.com

Walk that Walk
Quartier Général Press Office
71 Rue de la Fontaine au Roi
75011 Paris, France
Telephone: +33 143 38 80 70
Email: qg@quartier-general.com
www.quartier-general.com

Acknowledgments

Thank you

Paul Barton, Anna Burns, Jess Craven, Matt Doyle, Helen Evans, Graeme Fraser, Charlie Hanson, Catherine Hooper, Alan and Chris Huey, Allie Huey, Angus Hyland, Emma Jade, Maarit Niemelson, Elcee Orlova, Lara Ferros, Esther Teichmann, Georgina Thoms, Camilla Thomsen, Phoebe Watson and Andrew Wightman.